Demography and the Making of the Modern World

Demography and the Making of the Modern World

PUBLIC POLICIES AND DEMOGRAPHIC FORCES

John Rennie Short

© John Rennie Short 2024

This book is copyright under the Berne Convention.
No reproduction without permission.
All rights reserved.

First published in 2024 by Agenda Publishing

Agenda Publishing Limited
PO Box 185
Newcastle upon Tyne
NE20 2DH
www.agendapub.com

ISBN 978-1-78821-674-6 (hardcover)
ISBN 978-1-78821-704-0 (paperback)

British Library Cataloguing-in-Publication Data
A catalogue record for this book is available from the British Library

Typeset by JS Typesetting Ltd, Porthcawl, Mid Glamorgan
Printed and bound in the UK by CPI Group (UK) Ltd, Croydon, CR0 4YY

Contents

List of figures   vii

Introduction   1
1. The demographic transition model   5
2. Before the transition   13
3. The transition   27
4. The growing population   43
5. The bulging population   67
6. The shrinking population   87
7. The ageing population   107
8. Demographic narratives and moral panics   131
9. Demography and contemporary challenges   147

References   163
Index   167

Figures and Table

Figures

1.1	Stages of the demographic transition	8
2.1	The size of the world population over the long run	17
2.2	*The Dance of Death* (1493)	21
3.1	The Malthusian model	31
3.2	Children in the slums of Paris, 1913	35
3.3	Women at work in Busch Terminal, Brooklyn, USA, 1918	37
4.1	Infant mortality in the UK, 1930–2020	44
4.2	Population pyramid of Niger, 2020	53
4.3	China's total fertility rate, 1960–2014	58
4.4	Fertility and growth rates in Thailand	61
5.1	Population pyramid of Egypt, 2020	71
5.2	Population pyramid of China, 2020	74
5.3	Population pyramid of Bangladesh, 2020	81
6.1	Global fertility rate	88
6.2	US fertility rate, 1960–2021	89
7.1	Global population profile	108
7.2	Population pyramid of Japan, 2021	109
7.3	Life expectancy and healthcare spending	111
7.4	Old-age dependency ratio in USA	122
8.1	Global population projections	135

8.2	Teen births in the USA, 1991–2021	143
9.1	Population projections for Africa, Asia and Europe	151
9.2	Population projections for China, India, Russia and the USA	153

Table

7.1	Super-aged countries	107

Introduction

The aim of this book is to reveal the demographic forces that shape our modern world and evaluate the policies that have been devised to control and affect these forces.

The term *demography* was first used in a book by the Belgian Achille Guillard, published in 1855 under the title *Elements de statistique humaine ou demographie comparee* (*Elements of Human Statistics or Comparative Demography*). The term is now commonly used to refer to important trends such as rising population, ageing population and changes in life expectancy and birth rate. Demography is also a flourishing academic discipline producing a statistically sophisticated body of work. This book draws heavily on the work of professional demographers, clarified for a more general audience. However, the focus of this book is less on the statistical modelling of population trends and more on their economic, political and social implications.

Demographers sometimes use the term "vital statistics" to refer to population-related numbers. "Vital" has many meanings, but, for me, two stand out from the *Oxford English Dictionary*'s (*OED*) numerous definitions: "Imparting life or vigor" and "Supreme importance". The vital statistics of a society are, as the *OED* definitions imply, of "supreme importance". They are not simple reflections of social forces; they impart the life and vigour that help direct these changes. They are not just dependent variables. They are independent variables that play a significant role in shaping specific societies and global trends. Demography, in other words, is of great importance, perhaps best summed up in the phrase "Demography as Destiny". It is often attributed to Auguste Comte (1798–1857), but no formal citation has ever been found. Demography may in fact be destiny, but not in a simple mechanistic way. The relationships are often more subtle and elusive to the shallow analysis. We need to delve below the surface to reveal demography's powerful influence. But we should be wary of too mechanistic a narrative. The book avoids the simple causal argument that demography is the major source of all social changes but instead shows the complex interactions between social and demographic processes. The book highlights how demography is important but avoids the simplistic notion that it is a predetermined destiny.

In this book, I show how things as varied and important as the Arab Spring, migrant flights from Africa to Europe, budget negotiations in the USA, immigration debates in Japan and economic growth in India and Brazil, all seemingly diverse issues from around the world, are shaped by the forces of demography.

The book highlights the complex role of demography in creating the modern world. Many of the things that are taken for granted, such as the rise of the women's rights movement, calls for democratic participation, the rise and fall of populism and even bouts of xenophobic nationalism, are on closer examination deeply connected to demography. But demography has become a highly technical body of knowledge marked by careful data collection and statistical modelling. The siloing of social science research from broader discourses means that population issues are too often restricted to narrow academic debates while broader discussions about social issues rarely connect with the underlying demographic forces. Popular understandings of newsworthy social and political events rarely have time to explore their demographic basis. There is a definite gap between, on the one hand, demographers who like numbers but are uncomfortable with broader social and cultural theorizing and, on the other, social and cultural theorists who tend to be uncomfortable with numbers and public policy analysts who tend to focus too little attention on demographic issues. The book aims to fill this gap. It is concerned with a broader perspective that, drawing upon the experience of countries across the globe, makes clear the connection between demographic forces and social change. A particular focus of this book is the range of public policies that have been developed, rejected and adopted to meet these population challenges.

Chapter 1 introduces the reader to the idea of the demographic transition (DT). The basic DT model is outlined and the main effects are identified.

Chapter 2 sets the historical scene. The remaining chapters then follow the stages of the model. Chapter 3 examines the early stages of the transition. Chapter 4 looks at the forces behind the increase in life expectancy, the decline of mortality rates and the issue of rapid population growth. Chapter 5 evaluates the debates around the demographic dividend and the youth bulge. Chapter 6 looks at the impacts of a slowdown in population growth while Chapter 7 assesses the problems of ageing societies. The idea of the second DT is assessed. Chapter 8 frames contentious demographic issues as moral panics. Chapter 9 looks at the role of demography in climate change, global population redistribution and geopolitical shifts.

At the end of each chapter, I have included a range of books and articles that deal in more detail with some of the topics raised. Where I have specifically drawn on the work of other writers, I have cited their work in the text and given fuller bibliographic information in the References section at the end of the book. I have drawn on a wide variety of data sources. The main ones include Our World in Data (https://ourworldindata.org), Statista (https://www.statista.com), the United Nations (https://www.un.org/en/global-issues/population) and the World Population Review (https://worldpopulationreview.com).

FURTHER READING

There are many standard introductions to demography. Wolfgang Lutz's (2021) *Advanced Introduction to Demography* and Steven Murdock and David Ellis's *Applied Demography* (2019) are two of the more recent examples. They both provide a solid grounding in basic demography. There are also textbooks on population geography such as Bruce Newbold's *Population Geography* (2021, 4th edition), and Holly Barcus and Keith Halfacree's *An Introduction to Population Geographies: Lives across Space* (2017). Fewer studies take such a broad approach as this book does in discussing wider impacts, although exceptions include Tim Dyson's *Population and Development: The Development Transition* (2010), which looks at demography and economic development, Paul Morland's *The Human Tide: How Population Shaped the Modern World* (2019), which concentrates on the impact of the rapid population increase of the past 200 years, and Jennifer Sciubba's *A Research Agenda for Political Demography* (2021), which is an edited collection of scholarly articles. This book, in contrast to these volumes, highlights and evaluates the public policies devised to deal with the different stages of the transition.

1
The demographic transition model

Between 1800 and 1850 the human experience began to change. Before 1800, life was short and few made it into what we would now consider old age. Most women spent much of their life having and caring for children. The total human population was small, and with high mortality rates and low life expectancy, population growth was slow. After around 1850, major changes occurred, at first slowly and only in the richer countries, then more quickly as the transition diffused across the globe. Mortality rates declined, women had fewer children, people lived longer and the population increased.

Three basic statistics make the point. In 1700, the global average life expectancy was only 27 years of age; the global average fertility rate was six children per woman and only 4 per cent of the world's population was aged over 65. By 2020, the average life expectancy was 72 years of age, the average fertility rate was 2.4 and 9 per cent of the population was aged over 65. People lived longer, fertility rates fell and the population aged. This change is referred to as the 'demographic transition' or sometimes as the DT model. Remember, it is a model that simplifies the complex reality of the world. Demographic patterns before 1800 were more complex than the model posits. There were periods of rapid growth. In England, in the eighteenth century, as Tony Wrigley and colleagues have shown, there was a marked increase in marriage fertility and a consequent increase in population growth and in total population (Wrigley & Schofield 1989; Wrigley *et al.* 1997). War and famine reduced the population while peace and prosperity allowed population levels to rebound and grow.

There were also variations over space. Studies of both Belgium and Spain, for example, uncovered different fertility levels by region in the past and more recently. The differences are in part a result of varying levels of secularization, which is a reminder that variations in local cultures can produce marked differences in fertility levels (Lesthaeghe 1977; Lesthaeghe & Lopez-Gay 2013).

There are two important features to point out. First, there were and still are vast social differences behind global and even national averages. The rich tend to live longer than the poor. By mid-Victorian times in the UK, for example, the average middle-class man lived until 45 while the average working-class man died in his twenties. This 20-year difference in class has largely persisted down through the decades even as overall life expectancy has increased. Queen Victoria lived until she was 81, whereas most of her female subjects in England died at the age of 50. Her great-great granddaughter, Queen Elizabeth, died at the age of 96 in 2022, whereas her female subjects, on average, died at the age of 83. In the last years of her reign, her subjects in England's most deprived areas lived until 79 with a healthy life expectancy (years in good health) of only 52. Compared to the more affluent parts of the county, people living in the most deprived areas had 20 fewer years in good health (UK Government 2017; Office of National Statistics 2022). Demography embodies and reinforces differences in social class, wealth and power.

Second, the transition is a phenomenon that occurs at different times in different parts of the world. The broadest distinction is between rich and poor countries. The transition occurred first in Europe, then spread to the rest of the world. Let's look at just two statistics we introduced earlier: life expectancy and fertility rates. In 1800, no country had a life expectancy of more than 40 years of age. But by 1950, while the average Norwegian lived until they were 72, the average African lived only until aged 36. In Mali it was only 26. Differences persist. Life expectancy in Norway is now 82 years of age but is still only 60 in Mali. Similarly with fertility rates. In 1950, while Norway had on average 2.5 children per woman, the figure for Mexico was 6.7. By 2020, Norway's fertility rate was only 1.5 while Mexico has slumped to 1.8. The rates were converging. In Mali, in contrast, the decline was much less, from 6.9 in 1950 to 5.9 in 2020. Some areas of the world went through the transition at different times and more rapidly than others. And in some places, such as Nigeria, the transition appears to be blocked.

The DT has its limitations. It does not refer to household arrangements. If we concentrate on just traditional marriage arrangements, the age of the first marriage is an important factor in shaping the fertility rate and family size. Elizabeth Abot (2014) distinguishes three patterns in pre-transition Europe. In the West, men and women of similar ages married relatively late and established nuclear families. In the East, people tended to marry at a young age and joined existing households, most often the groom's extended family. In the Mediterranean region, young brides married older men because they tended to have inherited family property.

It is important to bear in mind that the DT is not a causal model. It describes the characteristics of the transition. It is descriptive and suggestive rather than causal and definitive. And while this does not invalidate its use, it does suggest some caution.

A MORE COMPLEX PICTURE

Figure 1.1 shows the DT in more detail as a series of different stages with corresponding population pyramids where population structure is divided by gender and age group. By convention the age cohorts are in five-year or ten-year intervals. At the outset, it is important to see the different stages as intellectual constructs. They are best understood as zones of transition rather than as fixed categorizations. The transition moves through the stages more as a continuous flow rather than as a series of discrete and contained categories. The stages in Figure 1.1 freeze what is in fact a continuous flow.

It begins, in stage 1, with the demographic characteristics of the premodern world before 1800–50. Birth rates and death rates are high and population increase is low. Few people live into old age. It has a population pyramid with a wide base that is sharply angled towards the top, quickly narrowing as the population ages. Old people constitute a small minority.

In stage 2, the death rates fall sharply. A combination of better nutrition and health care, often brought about by advances in medical technology, result in a rapid fall in rates, especially infant mortality. Because birth rates remain high there is a rapid increase in population. The pyramid becomes more of a triangle as more children live past infancy. In stage 3, both the mortality rates and

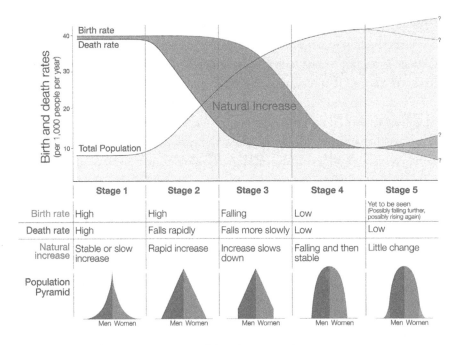

Figure 1.1 Stages of the demographic transition

Source: Max Roser, http://ourworldindata.org/data/population-growth-vital-statistics/world-population-growth. Reproduced under the CC BY-SA 4.0 licence.

birth rate begin to fall. Total population continues to increase but at a slower rate than in stage 2. The pyramid thickens at the lower levels as the decline in infant mortality first apparent in stage 2 begins to show up in more younger people as a proportion of the total population. The population pyramid begins to look like a haystack. In stages 2 and 3 the population surges. In stage 4, both birth and death rates are low. Population levels stabilize. The population pyramid looks like a gherkin as the large cohorts of younger people age through the years thickening at the top of the pyramid. The categorization of stage 5 – half present, half future – is more speculative. Life expectancy is high while birth rates may decline even more. The population ages and population growth levels off and may decline. The pyramid now more resembles a column as the different cohorts are roughly similar in size. The DT is a shift from a wide base with a sharp point to a more evenly shaped elongated bubble.

Some have even argued that stage 5 and beyond constitutes a second DT characterized by below replacement fertility and a variety of living conditions

– no longer the simple male–female marriage/relationship with children – including non-child married couples, single mothers and unmarried couples with and without children. Is this a distinctly different second DT or simply a continuation of stage 5? Lesthaeghe (2010) suggests a second DT. He points to the fact that, at least in the global North, after 1965 there are more single-person households, more divorce and more households in informal relations other than marriage.

EFFECTS OF THE TRANSITION

We can identify at least four major consequences of this transition. The first is a marked increase in population in stages 2 and 3 because of declining infant mortality and continuing birth rates. The very young begin to dominate the population profile. Second, as this large cohort ages, and fertility levels start to decline, stages 3 and 4 have more people in the middle years between youth and old age. This is known as the demographic bulge. Third, in stages 4 and 5, as population growth levels off with a marked decline in fertility, the population ages with an increasing proportion of people aged over 65. Over the course of the transition, the profile of the total population moves from youthful to middle aged to more elderly. Finally, the transition involves a massive and unprecedented increase in the human population. In 1800 the world population was one billion; by 2030 it will be 8.5 billion.

We explore these consequences in much greater detail in subsequent chapters.

ORIGINS OF THE MODEL

The idea of the DT, like all ideas about society, was shaped by a wider social context. The theory has its origins in the first half of the twentieth century but emerged more fully formed soon after the end of the Second World War. Two US demographers, Anlsey Coale and Edgar M. Hoover, poring over the population data from what were then called developing countries (the global

South) and especially the 1951 Census of India, concluded that high population growth was hampering economic development. Population growth would eventually decline with urbanization and industrialization, but simply waiting for a country to completely industrialize and modernize would be too late. It was deemed more efficient to tweak the fertility rate without having to wait for large-scale and slow-moving economic changes to unfold. Controlling population growth would unlock the economic potential of developing countries more quickly. This idea led to the promotion of government-sponsored policies of family planning. There was what one commentator described as a "pro-family planning activism amongst transition theorists" (Szreter 1993: 679). It initially received little official backing from the US government because of the opprobrium around birth control in the USA. But by the 1960s, against the background of Cold War competition, family planning was seen as a way for postcolonial countries to achieve development without the need for any radical changes such as land redistribution or taxes on the wealthy. The DT became the intellectual rationale for the rapid rise of family-planning programmes in aid packages.

The model was similar to other mechanistic models of economic development of the time, such as the Rostow model that imagined countries moving from traditional society, through the take-off, into modernization-industrialization and high mass consumption. It shared a similar ideological basis. The Rostow model assumed that underdevelopment was a natural condition that could be overcome with a commitment to modernization. It was the free market alternative to ideas about the development of underdevelopment caused by Western colonialism and global capitalism. It was an ideological counter to the idea that the world was structured by uneven progress that created development in some regions through the forced underdevelopment of other regions. The DT model had a similar ideological element. Since blame was easily assigned to the actions of the local population for having "too many" children, it was eagerly adopted in the rich West as it was a convenient way to avoid a fuller critique of the existing global economic-political order. The current DT model has shed many of these ideological trappings, but the bias in many of its earlier assumptions needs to be appreciated.

FURTHER READING

Classic studies of the DT model

Lee, R. 2003. "The demographic transition: three centuries of fundamental change". *Journal of Economic Perspectives* 17: 167–90.

Reher, D. 2004. "The demographic transition revisited as a global process". *Population, Space and Place* 10: 19–41.

Ruggles, S. 2015. "Patriarchy, power, and pay: the transformation of American families, 1800–2015". *Demography* 52: 1797–823.

The second demographic transition

Esteve, A., R. Lesthaeghe & A. López-Gay 2012. "The Latin American cohabitation boom, 1970–2007". *Population and Development Review* 38: 55–81.

Goldscheider, F., E. Bernhardt & T. Lapegård 2015. "The gender revolution: a framework for understanding changing family and demographic behavior". *Population and Development Review* 41: 207–39.

Zaidi, B. & S. Morgan 2017. "The second demographic transition theory: a review and appraisal". *Annual Review of Sociology* 43: 473.

Different aspects of the DT

Bocquier, R. & R. Costa 2015. "Which transition comes first? Urban and demographic transitions in Belgium and Sweden". *Demographic Research* 33: 1297–332.

Dribe, M., M. Oris & L. Pozzi 2014. "Socioeconomic status and fertility before, during and after the demographic transition: an introduction". *Demographic Research* 31: 161–82.

Reher, D. 2011. "Economic and social implications of the demographic transition". *Population and Development Review* 37: 11–33.

Intellectual history of the model

Kirk, D. 1996. "Demographic transition theory". *Population Studies* 50: 361–87.

Szreter, S. 1993. "The idea of demographic transition and the study of fertility change: a critical intellectual history". *Population and Development Review* 19: 659–701.

2
Before the transition

On the other side of the DT life was more fleeting. Most people lived directly off the land and were more reliant on the bounty of the earth and subject to the fluctuations in ecological conditions. This other world, in comparison to ours, had slower rates of growth, lower life expectancy and higher mortality rates, especially among children. It was a time of population vulnerability. The population lived on a knife's edge as even small deteriorations in living conditions could easily reduce population levels very quickly and sometimes almost to the point of annihilation. Rapid and large-scale population loss leads to the undermining of the basic functioning of society as lives were lost, keystone societal positions remained unfilled and cultural practices were wrecked. In this chapter I show how the consequences of this pre-transition demography shaped and continue to shape our present world.

THE GENETIC LEGACY OF POPULATION BOTTLENECKS

One legacy is that genetic characteristics of today's population are a result of previous bottlenecks. Population bottlenecks occur when there is a marked decline in the overall size of the population. They become more important the smaller and more isolated the population. Bottlenecks are caused by war and famine, disease, pandemics and the collapse of environmental support systems.

It is now generally agreed that the human population originated in Africa. From 100,000 years ago, small groups of migrants left Africa in successive waves to settle the world. It is estimated that fewer than 6,000 people were part of the first wave. They constituted just a small part of the genetic diversity of the total African population. The difference remains to this day so that the farther a traditional group lives away from Africa the less the genetic diversity. Ashraf and Galor (2013) propose an interesting idea: that there is an optimum level of diversity for long-term economic growth. Too much genetic diversity, as in the case of Africa, can lead to lack of cooperation. Too little diversity, as the case of the Americas, can lead to lower levels of innovation. They tested their hypothesis on conditions before colonialism, to concentrate on endogenous rather than exogenous factors, and used population density as a proxy for the level of development. They concluded that an increase in diversity in more homogeneous societies and a decrease in more heterogeneous societies led to an increase in population density. The results are more suggestive than conclusive, so their hypothesis remains more of an intriguing possibility than an established fact. However, they do point out the possibility that genetic diversity may have played a role in precolonial development patterns and shaped the global variation in economic growth.

The giant volcanic explosion of Toba that occurred 70,000 years ago caused another population bottleneck. The volcanic eruption was huge. Nothing like it has occurred since. The lava flows covered 20,000 km^2. The volcano spewed out the dense rock equivalent of volcanic ash of 800 km^3. Krakatoa in contrast erupted 15 km^3. Toba was 53 times more powerful and created a volcanic winter as sunlight was reduced, temperatures fell and living conditions worsened. Rough estimates suggest that the world population may have decreased from 2.5 million to fewer than 10,000. The remaining population was scattered in small, isolated groups that began to genetically differentiate because of founder effects that occur when isolated communities reduce generic diversity inside the group but differentiate more from other groups. Toba's volcanic winter helped to create the differentiation of the human population. Subsequently, this genetically diverse population adapted to local environments. This came with benefits but also costs. The population at higher altitudes evolved to resist hypoxia (a condition of dangerously low levels of oxygen in body tissues) but that made them more vulnerable to pulmonary hypertension. In food-scarce central Australia the inhabitants developed a fat storage mechanism that coped with a variable food supply but that in turn led to greater prevalence of type 2 diabetes. Traditional Europeans evolved traits of modulation of immune system sensitivity to contend with pathogens but that made them more prone to autoimmune and inflammatory disorders and, as it happens, at greater risk of fatality from Covid-19 (Benton *et al.* 2021).

Another bottleneck occurred around 20,000 years ago when people moved from Siberia across the Bering Strait. A series of small waves populated the New World. This population had little genetic diversity, which made it less resistant to specific diseases and more vulnerable to epidemics and pandemics. The arrival of Europeans was a demographic calamity. The early colonists transmitted diseases such as measles and influenza, which for them were everyday occurrences but fatal for the more vulnerable New World population. The entry of new, highly contagious diseases into a homogenously genetic population with no natural immunity created the demographic holocaust involving the loss of 90 per cent of the original inhabitants (Thornton 1987). The relatively easy and quick European colonization of the New World was based on these demographic differences.

In the more distant past, when the global population was much smaller, bottlenecks played a significant role in shaping our genetic composition that in turn impacted differential susceptibility to disease, the pace of colonial appropriations and perhaps even long-term differences in global economic development. There is even a contemporary legacy in variations to the impact of Covid-19. However, it is important to factor in the role of socioeconomic conditions when we compare the Covid-19 death rates of ethnic and racial minorities in specific countries. Comorbidities such as poorer living conditions and unequal access to health care are an important part of the health outcome differences between racial and ethnic groups in individual countries (Golestaneh *et al.* 2020).

THE RISE AND FALL OF POPULATIONS

As the world population steadily increased, the risk of global bottlenecks decreased. More people spread across the world meant a large enough base-level population to avoid catastrophic global population crashes. And as we got closer to the present there was less possibility for evolutionary genetic changes. However, regional populations could fall, often with dramatic results; not enough in most cases to change genetic make-up but substantial enough to influence societal structures and cultural practices.

At the end of the Pleistocene, commonly known as the Ice Age, there was a rapid series of warmings as the earth gradually broke free from an icy grip. Ecological conditions changed rapidly, especially at the edge of the receding glaciation. Unlike the tropical areas of the world that were less impacted by the glacial conditions, change in Europe was more dramatic. One study estimates that the population in Europe between 30,000 years and 13,000 years ago fluctuated between 130,000 and 410,000 (Tallavaara *et al.* 2015). In the warmer, wetter conditions trees flourished, creating more habitats for animals and birds. The warmer seas and rivers provided more shellfish. For hunter-gatherer societies this increase in the food supply meant less infant mortality. A more detailed study of Iberia found that the hunter-gatherer population rebounded quickly during warming periods (Fernández-López de Pablo *et al.* 2019).

As temperatures stabilized and the world warmed the human population began to grow and expand across the globe. Figure 2.1 shows the global population over the long term. The figures are estimates because it is only since the eighteenth and nineteenth centuries that, with the more formal counting of the population, more reliable estimates are possible. Despite this proviso, over most of human history the total human population was small with very low growth rates. By 7,000 years ago, the world population had increased to between 5 and 20 million people. It was now reaching escape velocity from the immediate threat of annihilation. The human population thickened and spread so that human survival seemed relatively more secure. Over the next thousand years the population increased to between 170 and 400 million (US Census 2022).

But against the general trend for the human population to increase there were local events that had dramatic consequences. Among the many, we can consider the case of Athens, where between 430 and 427 BCE the city state lost almost a quarter of its population to typhus. Most of the city population was infected, including the great historian Thucydides, who survived to comment in his *History of the Peloponnesian War* that the catastrophe was so overwhelming that "men, not knowing what would happen next to them, became indifferent to every rule of religion or law".

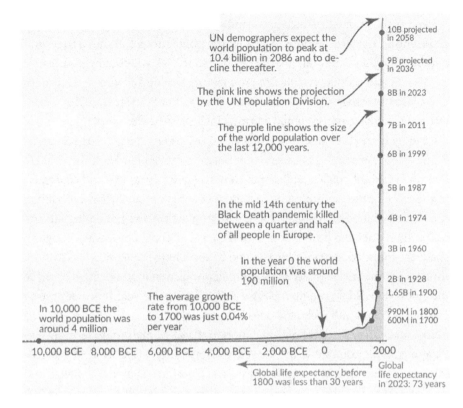

Figure 2.1 The size of the world population over the long run

Source: Max Roser, OurWorldinData.org (https://ourworldindata.org/population-growth-over-time). Reproduced under the CC BY 4.0 DEED licence https://creativecommons.org/licenses/by/4.0/.

Notes: based on estimates by the History Database of the Global Environment and the United Nations.

The experience of suddenly high death rates can generate a form of hysteria or moral panic. The traditional deities seem to abandon the people. Scapegoats are identified. The "other" is to blame. Prior to the plague, Athens was one of the more open city states and receptive to strangers. After the plague, the city restricted admission to citizenship. The epidemic weakened Athens just as it was warring with its traditional foe, Sparta. The Athenians lost the Peloponnesian War and never again regained their pivotal position in ancient Greece.

Even as the population increased, and settled agriculture replaced hunting-gathering across large swathes of the world, populations continued to be vulnerable. The Late Antiquity Ice Age from 536 to 660, when temperatures fell by 2.5°C below normal, resulted in crop failure, famine and widespread social dislocation. A variety of imperial reshufflings and political turmoil have been attributed to this environmental collapse, including the westward migration of the Mongols and the rapid spread of Islam (Key 2000). The fall of the Sassanid Empire, for example, was caused by population movement from the Arabian Peninsula and the Asian steppes that were triggered by famine and epidemics in the wake of the environmental changes (Büntgen *et al.* 2016: Matloubkari & Shaikh Baikloo Islam 2022). The loss of population was not enough to significantly reduce the population as in the case of Toba, but it was enough to shake the foundation of existing societies. Even where population loss was not threatening the survivability of the human population it was enough to shake the status quo. Rapid population loss is like a corrosive acid that can destroy existing societies and etch new ones in their wake.

In some cases, the level of population loss was enough to undermine civilizations. One example is the Mayan Collapse. The Maya lived in the area in Central America which now consists of Yucatan, Guatemala, Belize and southern Mexico. The Classical Mayan civilization lasted from around 200 to 1000 CE. Their cities include Tikal and Uaxactun, Chichen Itza, Mayapan, Copan and Palenque. Tikal's population is estimated to have been around 60,000, giving it a population density several times greater than the average European city at the same time in history. The Maya were highly accomplished in astronomy with an intimate knowledge of the calendar. The cosmology of the Maya permeated their lives and structured their cities. Cities were designed to coincide with astronomical rhythms. At Chichen Itza, on the day of the spring and autumn equinox, during sunset, a sun serpent rises on the side of the stairway of the pyramid called El Castillo. In Mayan sites in the central and southern lowlands many temples have doorways and other features that align to celestial events. The Mayan civilization lasted for over 800 years because of their creative use of resource management and food production techniques (Seligson, 2023). Yet, despite their ingenuity, beginning in the eighth century and continuing for some 150 years, the great Mayan cities were abandoned as wars raged and people fled. One important cause was a megadrought, a prolonged period of significantly less precipitation. To support both farms and cities of 60,000–100,000 people, the Maya had to cut down forests and increasingly manipulate wetlands. These actions consumed water that could not be spared during periods of drought. The Maya also unintentionally made their own agriculture less productive with their extensive deforestation. Removing trees stopped the cycle by which the tree canopy would capture and return the naturally occurring nutrient phosphorus to the soil (Turner 2020). The people, unable to live off the parched and desiccated land, moved away, leaving the cities to be overcome by jungle. Tropical vegetation ended up enveloping the once vibrant cities.

The Black Death

Perhaps the greatest decline in human population in relatively recent years was caused by the Black Death. This was the name given to a bubonic plague epidemic that swept across Eurasia and North Africa. Those affected experienced flu-like symptoms, then outbreaks of pus-filled pustules around the armpits and groins. Most died in extreme pain within a week. It is estimated to have killed at least a third of the global population. By 1340 the world population is estimated at around 443 million. It had grown substantially over the previous decades, with warmer temperatures and more bounteous harvests, but after the Black Death, by 1400 the world's population had fallen to 374 million (see Figure 2.1). In Europe, the effect was devastating where it first appeared in Messina in Sicily in October 1347 when a trading ship landed with diseased sailors. By January 1348 it had spread to France and North Africa, by 1349 it reached Paris and by 1351 it covered all of Europe. The death rate was enormous. Through 1349 the death rate in Paris was 800 a day. Florence lost 65 per cent of its citizens, Pisa 70 per cent. In one village in Cambridgeshire in England the death rate was 70 per cent. The English children's nursery rhyme "Ring a Ring o' Roses" may have its origins in the Black Death with its fateful last line, "We all fall down".

It seemed like the end of the world. Crowds of barefoot penitents wandered the land beating themselves with whips. Local Jewish populations were blamed for the pestilence: it was widely believed that they had poisoned the drinking water. In 1348 the first lynching occurred. In towns and cities across the continent, Jewish property was confiscated and Jews were thrown into bonfires.

The impact in Europe was devastating as almost half of the population died in just a few years. The plague erupted six times over the next six decades, reducing the population further. Europe did not reach its 1300 population again until 1500. The impacts of such a huge loss of life in such a short period of time are immense. Religion provided little comfort. Neither prayers nor virtue guaranteed immunity from the disease. Bishops and cardinals succumbed as well as peasants and farmers; priest and prelate as well as labourer and blacksmith. Existing medical practices were unable to comprehend let alone treat the illness.

The effects disrupted the existing society. The huge and rapid death rate meant there was less labour to work the land. The relationship between lord and master was transformed as some peasants got richer after they inherited the holdings of dead family members. Peasants and smallholding tenant farmers could demand higher wages and cheaper rents. With more land, lower rents and higher wages, the Black Death opened up new opportunities for those on the lower rungs of society. The Black Death undermined the remaining remnants of feudalism and ushered in a more modern, capitalist society.

The Black Death also created a pervasive sense of death that influenced art forms. The presence of death was visualized in frescoes, statues and painting. The impermanence of life and the ever present certainty of death became recurring motifs. Stone effigies of decaying corpses, woodcuts of dancing skeletons and the Danse Macabre, and recurring images in paintings of skulls, wilted flowers and decaying food, all gave aesthetic form to the pronounced sense of mortality. Figure 2.2, entitled *The Dance of Death*, by Michael Wolgemut in the *Nuremburg Chronicle*, first published in 1493, is a common motif of the era. Art was infused with *memento mori*, constant reminders of decay and death. New, dark genres became part of a new more morbid art. Some of the themes persisted down through the years, from Frans Hals to Paul Cezanne, who depicted piles of skulls. Van Gogh painted a skull smoking a cigarette. The plague centred death and dying as subjects of art. Before the plague, death was often depicted as a brief passage to a heaven, afterwards it was a subject in its own right, a constant presence in the artistic imagination. Post-plague art became obsessed with death and sin.

Even architecture was impacted as in the shift towards the perpendicular style away from the more florid, opulent ornamentation of French gothic. The loss of population meant fewer workers with the necessary skills to do the

Figure 2.2 *The Dance of Death* by Michael Wolgemut, from the *Nuremberg Chronicle* by Hartmann Schedel (1493)

Source: https://commons.wikimedia.org/wiki/File:Nuremberg_chronicles_-_Dance_of_Death_(CCLXIIIIv).jpg.

delicate decorative work of French gothic. The economic recession in the wake of the pandemic also limited architectural ornamentation.

The Black Death undermined religious authority, medical expertise, social hierarchies and established customs. The scale and pace of death shook the foundation of society and by weakening the established order paved the way for the more inquiring, sceptical and critical thinking of the Renaissance.

The Black Death was the strongest selection event in recent history. The scale of death was enough to affect a noticeable genetic legacy. A recent study using the teeth of ancient skeletons before, during and after the plague found that people with a specific genetic mutation that encouraged resilience had a 40 per cent higher chance of surviving the disease. This mutation was carried over to future generations and the plague-resistant mutations are more common today than they were before the Black Death. However, these protective genes also make people more susceptible to inflammatory autoimmune diseases such as Crohn's disease (Klunk *et al.* 2022). We still carry around the genetic consequences of the Black Death.

The Black Death was only the beginning of a worldwide pandemic, or cyclical series of epidemics, recurring at intervals of 2–20 years throughout Europe until well into the seventeenth century. A brief, favourable economic environment thus seems to have been a precondition for the Renaissance in culture, art and politics and the spread of new kinds of consumer demand. Then, from the middle of the fifteenth century, living standards gradually worsened and eventually reached the low levels that had prevailed prior to the Renaissance.

Demographic holocaust in the New World

It is now generally agreed that the first human settlers of the New World came across from Siberia between 17,000 and 23,000 years ago. They left the Old World before the domestication of animals. So, unlike the later generations of the Old World of Africa, Asia and Europe, they did not live beside domesticated animals and thus did not build up an immunity to the many diseases transmitted by these animals such as influenza, smallpox, measles and chickenpox. When Europeans came to the New World they brought with them germs and diseases that were fatal to the local populations. Estimates suggest that there were almost 54 million people in the New World on the eve of the entry of Europeans in 1492. By 1650 the population had declined to just over five million. It was a tragedy of epic proportions as entire populations succumbed to disease and death. Whole tribes died. Languages were lost and cultures destroyed. The demographic collapse had environmental consequences. There was a reduction in managed burning and so the forest recovered, and the numbers of previously hunted animals rebounded. Later European explorers and settlers saw and described a pristine wilderness that was, in fact, a regenerated wilderness that had been created by the eradication of much of its indigenous population.

The Little Ice Age

There was one more global catastrophe. We are not exactly sure what caused it, but after a slight cooling around 1300, significant cooling started in 1570 and lasted for about 110 years, only warming up significantly around 1800. It involved a global cooling of around 2°C and a series of brutal winters. Agricultural productivity plummeted and famine stalked the land. World population declined by a third with some areas such as China experiencing a 50 per cent decline. The cooling disrupted the grain harvest, and this resulted in food riots, panics and rebellions. There was a vicious cycle as peasants went hungry and could not pay their rents. Landlords were pinched for money and town dwellers had to pay more for their daily bread. There were immediate and longer-term impacts. The cooling impacted individual events such as the 1588 destruction of the Spanish Armada caused by Arctic hurricanes. Without the cooling, the Armada may have succeeded in the invasion of England and in the installing of a Catholic monarchy. In the longer term, the cooling and fall-off in local food supplies meant merchants had to look further afield to find enough food. Longer-distance trade was stimulated to obtain grain. These new trade routes led to the growth of a money economy and the rise of strategically located merchant cities. The rise of Amsterdam as a trading city owes its origins to many factors but the rise of its grain trade and money transactions are important. In a more global perspective, the historian Geoffrey Parker (2013) argues that the seventeenth-century plague of revolts, rebellions and revolutions were caused, in part, by the population losses and social dislocations brought about by the Little Ice Age. But as with the Black Death, the catastrophe was the antechamber for a new order. Philipp Blom (2019) argues that the Little Ice Age also ultimately led to industrialization, societal upheavals and mass migrations, a gradual weaning from traditional religions, the birth of the Enlightenment and the dawn of the industrial revolution.

SUMMARY

Demography plays a large part in human history. In the longer term, our genetic make-up owes a great deal to the population bottlenecks of a bygone time. In the more medium term, such significant historical events as the fall of ancient empires, the creation of new forms of social order (e.g. the shift from feudalism to capitalism), the development of new trade routes and the defeat of the indigenous population of the New World have a strong demographic component that is only now being uncovered. In the shorter term, demographic changes and ruptures played a role in major upheavals such as the Renaissance, the Enlightenment and the industrial revolution. Their emergence is not only because of the catastrophic population loss of the Black Death or the Little Ice Age, but they did play a role, and one that we are only just discovering. Because of our relatively recent interest in climate change and the contemporary impact of pandemics, we are only now beginning to reorient our historical sensitivity to how the modern world was created and shaped. Demography plays a more significant role than traditional historiography has assigned.

The main takeaway: demographic changes, especially rapid and unsettling changes, are significant factors in important large-scale social and cultural changes, economic transformations and political upheavals.

FURTHER READING

Genetic bottlenecks

Ambrose, S. 1998. "Late Pleistocene human population bottlenecks, volcanic winter, and differentiation of modern humans". *Journal of Human Evolution* 34: 623–51.

Amos, W. & J. Hoffman 2010. "Evidence that two main bottleneck events shaped modern human genetic diversity". *Proceedings of the Royal Society B: Biological Sciences* 277: 131–7.

Late Antiquity Ice Age 536–660

Keys, D. 2000. *Catastrophe: An Investigation into the Origins of the Modern World*. New York: Ballantine.

Rosen, W. 2007. *Justinian's Flea: The First Great Plague and the End of the Roman Empire*. New York: Penguin.

The Black Death

Bailey, M. 2021. *After the Black Death: Economy, Society, and the Law in Fourteenth-Century England*. Oxford: Oxford University Press.

Benedictow, O. 2004. *The Black Death, 1346–1353: The Complete History*. Woodbridge: Boydell.

Cantor, N. 2015. *In the Wake of the Plague: The Black Death and the World It Made*. New York: Simon & Schuster.

Cohn, S. 1997. *The Cult of Remembrance and the Black Death: Six Renaissance Cities in Central Italy*. Baltimore, MD: Johns Hopkins University Press.

Dodds, B. 2022. *Myths and Memories of the Black Death*. Cham, CH: Springer Nature.

Jedwab, R., N. Johnson & M. Koyama 2022. "The economic impact of the Black Death". *Journal of Economic Literature* 60: 132–78.

The demographic holocaust

Denevan, W. 1992. "The pristine myth: the landscape of the Americas in 1492". *Annals of the Association of American Geographers* 82(3): 369–85.

Thornton, R. 1987. *American Indian Holocaust and Survival: A Population History since 1492*. Norman: University of Oklahoma Press.

The Little Ice Age, 1570–1680

Appleby, A. 1980. "Epidemics and famine in the Little Ice Age". *Journal of Interdisciplinary History* 10(4): 643–63.

Blom, P. 2019. *Nature's Mutiny: How the Little Ice Age of the Long Seventeenth Century Transformed the West and Shaped the Present*. New York: Liveright Publishing.

Mann, M. 2002. "Little Ice Age". *Encyclopedia of Global Environmental Change* 1(504): e509.

Parker, G. 2013. *Global Crisis: War, Climate Change and Catastrophe in the Seventeenth Century*. New Haven, CT: Yale University Press.

3
The transition

POOR, NASTY, BRUTISH AND SHORT

The philosopher Thomas Hobbes (1588–1679) is credited with the description of life as "poor, nasty, brutish and short". It was a pithy description employed to highlight a life lived outside of society and part of his argument for a social contract to ensure social peace. In contrast to the lauding of the state of nature by the French philosopher Jean-Jacques Rousseau (1712–78), who argued we are born free but everywhere in chains, Hobbes posited the need for a social contract because, in a state of nature, there would be "[n]o arts, no letters; no society; and which is worst of all, continual fear, and danger of violent death; and the life of man, solitary, poor, nasty, brutish and short". His last four adjectives could well be used to describe the lot of most people before the DT. It was a time of high infant mortality, low life expectancy, poor nutrition and inadequate medical care. When Hobbes published his book *Leviathan* in 1651, from which the quotes are taken, the average life expectancy in England was 43 years, and six out of ten children died before they reached adulthood. Women gave birth to between five and eight children and in most cases only reared four to early adulthood. One in eight women died giving birth.

Population growth was slow and subject to fluctuations as failed harvests, social chaos, war and disruption could increase mortality. The Black Death and the Little Ice Age led to population decreases across the globe with instances of very marked population decline at the more regional level.

There were cultural consequences of this demographic situation. Death was a common presence; many children died in childbirth and people did not live very long. Our ancestors were surrounded by death in their everyday lives. The presence of death did not make the loss any less wrenching. Traditional societies had complex mourning rituals to cope with the loss of loved ones. Australian Aborigines, for example, had weeks, sometimes months, of ceremonies and rituals, called "sorry business". But the constant presence of death meant that it could never be ignored and had to be accommodated into cultural practices and belief systems. In the Viking sagas, for example, a warrior's death was not the end of life but the entry into Valhalla. For the ancient Greeks the search for glory in war and athletic prowess was actively pursued as a way for your name to live on. According to Greek legend, Achilles was offered a choice by the gods of a long and peaceful life or a short one filled with glory. Like many Greeks of the day, he went for the glory. In a very short-lived life, why not?

Major religions also wanted to attract followers with the promise of extending life beyond the limited lifespan. Both Christianity and Islam saw death, at least for the righteous, as the avenue to an everlasting life in a glorious and deathless hereafter. For short lives filled with the presence of death, the possibility of a wondrous and eternal hereafter was a way to cope with the reality of a nasty, brutish and short life.

The demography before the transition had a low reproductive efficiency. With high infant mortality and short lives, most women had to spend most of their lives having and caring for children. The emphasis was on each woman having as many children as possible. This demography reinforced patriarchy: the belief system and practice that men are authority figures and women should be restricted to the home, the hearth and the bearing and rearing of children. The emergence and reinforcement of patriarchal attitudes is one of the consequences of life before the transition. Another is the attitude towards children and old people. When many children die at birth or soon afterwards, each newborn is treated with love but also some measure of hesitation and trepidation. Families in traditional Korea would only celebrate the birth and name the child after 100 days. Very young babies were considered to be extremely vulnerable and, when things got tough, expendable. There are numerous cases of child infanticide in societies across the world during hard times. Today, infanticide is considered a horrible crime. Yet it persists where there are difficult conditions for mothers in a punitive patriarchy. In Senegal, a poor country with few child health facilities and limited birth control, almost 20 per cent of females in prison are charged with infanticide (Newman 2019).

Living to old age was a rare event in societies before the transition. Most people died before reaching 50 years of age. Those few who lived much longer generated tremendous respect. In traditional societies where the rate of technological progress was slow, the aged could pass on useful knowledge to the younger generations. Respect and obedience to the elderly is particularly strong in Confucian-inflected societies. In China, birthday celebrations grow in importance and size after the age of 60. Ingrained respect for elders remains in many societies. In the Philippines, many shops and banks still have signs that allow the elderly to pass to the front of the line.

After the transition, and closer to the present day, we can sometimes see a reversal of these attitudes. As technological progress quickens the elderly become less a source of wisdom. In many cases, grandchildren now must tell their grandparents how things work. And when there are significant transfers of resources to an expanding elderly population from a shrinking working population, then the elderly may become as much a burden as a blessing. With more older people both in absolute and relative terms, and especially if they are recipients of welfare payments funded by the working population, reverence can easily evaporate to be replaced by a mixture of envy and resentment. Attitudes towards the elderly are changing, albeit slowly, especially in more traditional societies. But across the world the elderly are losing the privileged cultural position they once held.

Similarly, attitudes towards children have also changed in the richer parts of the world, where most children live long past infancy. No longer so vulnerable, expendable or replaceable, they take on special importance. Nowhere was this changing attention so obvious as in the one-child policy of China where, especially for the urban middle class, the single male child was treated so well that the term *little emperor* was used to suggest their privileged existence as the singular point of attention for two parents and four grandparents.

Even the terms "children" and "elderly" take on different meanings before and after the transition. Before the transition, life was compressed, and after a very brief period of childhood most people moved quickly into adulthood. The many stages employed in our contemporary world, such as childhood, adolescence and young adult, had less relevance. The ideas of the innocence of childhood, the rebellious teen and the sullen adolescent are a product of the modern, post-transition world. Even the seven ages of man noted in Shakespeare's *As You Like It* (1623) only has infant, schoolboy, then different careers on the slide into old age, and for most people in Elizabethan England, the school part was either very brief or non-existent. Today, phrases such as "60 is the new 40" are suggestive of the expanded horizons for those previously just considered old. There were more children than old people. Before the transition, because of more restricted life expectancy few people lived long enough to become grandparents and rarer still to have adult grandchildren. The grandparent–grandchild nexus only becomes common after the transition.

MALTHUSIAN MELANCHOLY

It is perhaps ironic that on the eve of the transition that would change the world, a profoundly pre-transition tract was written. It is even more ironic that it would come to exercise such a strong influence long after its usefulness had ended.

Thomas Malthus was born in 1766, one of eight children born to a prosperous middle-class family in Surrey, England. He lived through two major events that shaped his view of the world. The first was a rare demographic occasion in English history – a decline in mortality in England – which started in the 1730s and was accompanied by a steady increase in fertility rates until 1800. He was thus writing at a rare time of rising birth rates and increasing population growth. Second, across the Channel the French Revolution had upturned the social order and inaugurated a more radical critique of the established hierarchy in England and across Europe. Social conservatives, such as Malthus, were distrustful of social change and sceptical about the idea of upward progress. In his most famous work, *An Essay on the Principles of Population*, which he worked on over six successive editions from 1798 to 1826, he argued that while population increased at a geometric rate, food supply only grows at an arithmetic rate. When times are good, people have more children. But the population increases eventually overshoot the available food supply until misery, poverty and famine – so-called Malthusian checks – force families to respond by having fewer children. The population then decreases, bringing population growth back into alignment with the food supply. The basic argument is outlined in Figure 3.1.

There were social implications to his model. Malthus was a social conservative who argued that policies aimed at helping the poor, such as social welfare, which enabled the poor to have children, simply made things worse. He believed that the number of children born to the poor should be limited. It is an idea that appears again and again in the demographic literature, social debates and political arguments right up until the present day. It is one of the great zombie ideas of demography, ideas that no longer have explanatory purchase but simply refuse to die.

Malthus's ideas had a significant impact both in Britain and across the world. In Britain his ideas influenced contemporary politicians who introduced the census in 1801 as a means of counting the population. He was an unwitting father of biopolitics. His ideas also influenced social legislation such as the New Poor Law of 1834 that created punishing workhouses for the poor.

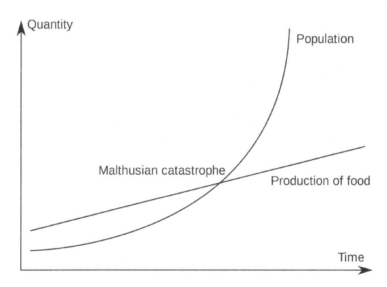

Figure 3.1 The Malthusian model

Source: Wikimedia Commons (https://commons.wikimedia.org/wiki/File:Malthus_PL_en.svg). Licensed under the Creative Commons Attribution-Share Alike 3.0 Unported license.

His ideas filtered out to social theorists such as Herbert Spencer (1820–1903), who espoused a social Darwinism based on the idea of "survival of the fittest". The phrase, often associated with Charles Darwin, originates with Spencer. More generally, Malthus's basic idea diffused across the world: there are too many people for the available resources and government should not interfere with the "natural" mechanism of Malthusian checks. There is also the often unspoken assumption that it is the poorest that are the problem. Always, it seems, it is the poor, the marginal and the powerless that are having too many children. Not me. Not us. Them.

His beliefs did not go unchallenged. He was roundly criticized in the radical working-class journals of the day and in 1820 William Godwin calculated that the world's population could comfortably reach nine billion. At the time he was writing, the population was little more than one billion and few could imagine today's population of over eight billion. But most people tend to remember Malthus's gloomy prediction rather than Godwin's sunnier outlook.

His ideas reverberated down the years. Hitler's *Mein Kampf* is filled with Malthusian ideas encased in social Darwinism and racial hatred. In Hitler's view, the world was divided into races competing for resources and dominance. The Jews were evildoers out to dominate the world order. It was a struggle to the death. He also believed, despite contemporary evidence to the contrary, that food supply was limited. He also drew on recent history. The UK could and had used its naval power to block food imports into Germany. Rivals could starve Germany. There was also the experience of the USA. Land appropriation, ethnic cleansing and subsequent land colonization provided vast lands and secure food that enabled the global rise of the USA. So why not for Germany? The lands that beckoned Hitler eyes were eastwards in the land populated by Slavs and Jews. Food supplies for the German people could only be guaranteed with the conquests of this fertile territory. Germans needed this *lebensraum* (living space) to survive and prosper. It is too much of a stretch to blame Hitler directly on Malthus. But the basic idea that food supply was limited fed directly into the idea that ensuring food supply could be increased by the annexation of territory, with its darkest expression in Hitler's strategy to appropriate land in eastern Europe with the ethnic cleansing of Jews and Slavs.

Malthus's ideas are also employed to explain famine. Most work on famine points to the fact that it is rarely about the lack of food supply and more about the distribution of food. Global hunger is not inevitable, and even as the global population has increased hunger is not a necessary corollary. The number of undernourished people in the world fell from over a billion in 1992 to 792 million in 2015 even as the population increased from 5.4 to 7.5 billion. Despite this, a Malthusian melancholy lingers on. The idea that population can and often will overshoot the available resources, especially food, appears again and again in national and global debates. Written at a specific time, his arguments continue to resonate to this day and simply will not die, despite all evidence to the contrary.

THE CONTEXT TO THE TRANSITION

The period from 1800 to 1850 marks the first stirrings of the transition. As shown in Figure 2.1, it is also when the world's population began its precipitous increase. This demographic shift is associated with four other major trends: the agricultural revolution, the industrial revolution, urbanization and biopolitics. The relationship between the DT and these trends is complex, braided and multidimensional with cause and effect flowing both ways that resulted in the dramatic rise of population.

The agricultural revolution

Consider the case of England and Wales, where the population increased from 5.5 million in 1700 to over 9 million in 1801. The increase was in part because of increases in agricultural output against a background of warming with the end of the Little Ice Age. The agricultural revolution took place in the series of waves of innovation from the mid-seventeenth century to the late nineteenth century. Innovations, such as the use of crop rotation to allow fields to lie fallow and regain fertility, allowed the intensive cultivation of light soils. New crops such as the potato, introduced from the New World, produced three times more calories per acre than the traditional cereals of wheat and barley. There were improvements in the plough and more effective land conversion, drainage and reclamation and livestock breeding. The enclosure movement, which removed the common rights of villagers in a privatization of collective land, allowed greater capital investment. A rural peasantry was replaced by a more capitalistic agriculture. Although relatively small, the British national market was one of the most spatially integrated. The lack of tariffs meant there were few barriers to commercial movement across the national space and trade was helped by declines in transportation costs brought about by improvement of roads and inland waterways.

Subsequent global waves of innovation in agricultural production throughout the nineteenth century reduced the need for agricultural labour, increased the food supply and laid the basis for economic growth. Fewer workers could provide food for more people. Productivity gains meant a decline in the demand for agricultural labour.

The industrial revolution

The agricultural revolution paved the way for the industrial revolution. From around 1760 to 1840, this revolution was associated with the rise of capitalism, as it was dependent on private investment rather than government control. Capitalism saw its full emergence with the industrial revolution.

Colonialism and imperialism also played a major part because colonies provided cheap raw materials and a guaranteed market for finished goods. There was a transfer of wealth from the colonial peripheries to the imperial cores. The uneven development of the world had its origins in the exploitation of the colonies by the colonizers.

The development of new energy sources was also important. There are many reasons behind Britain's early prominence and industrial revolution but the presence of coal, and especially coal relatively close to the surface and therefore easy to mine and extract, was a significant reason. This new and relatively cheap energy source powered the steam engines that were used to create new forms of transportation and new types of machinery.

The agricultural revolution both increased the food supply and created a large pool of excess labour that could be employed in the expanding factories and new mines. The shift from an agrarian economy to a manufacturing economy led to migration from rural areas to urban areas and increased the demand for skilled labour. Subsequent economic development increased demand for ever more skilled labour.

Urbanization

While agricultural revolutions decrease the demand for labour, industrial revolutions increase the demand. The result is rapid urbanization. The early industrial cities were dangerous. With people living at high densities, often with minimal or no public health, in unsanitary conditions, disease was constant and death was common. Figure 3.2 shows the poor living conditions for children in the slums of Paris in 1913. Cities were sinks of disease and death. Mortality levels in the first industrialized cities of Europe were higher than in the rural areas (Lynch 2003). Between the fifteenth and eighteenth centuries, farm families in English counties had twice as many surviving children as London families. In many countries up until around 1850, the urban death threat was higher than the urban birth rate. Urban growth was only maintained by high levels of rural to urban migration as people sought jobs and new

Figure 3.2 Children in the slums of Paris, 1913

Source: Bibliothèque nationale de France, https://commons.wikimedia.org/wiki/File:Les_enfants_de_la_zone_(Ivry,_1913).jpeg.

opportunities. Eventually, with better public health, mortality rates evened out. The urban birth rate became higher than the urban death rate and so city populations grew. By the turn of the twentieth century there was only a small difference in mortality between rural and urban areas in England. Thereafter, mortality rates fell faster in urban areas than rural areas because of greater access to medical care and better public health.

Three changes in the job market reinforced the DT. First, urban labour markets tended to value skill and expertise. Emphasis was thus placed on skill accumulation and since it was easier to devote resources to fewer rather than more children, and over the longer term urban households tended to have fewer children. Urban households shifted their emphasis from child quantity to child quality. We have contemporary evidence of this trade-off. One study showed that in Vietnam, with improvements in education, households decided to invest more in the quality of an individual child's life over the number of children (Dang & Rogers 2016). With fewer children there is more investment per child and more human capital, and so per capita income growth can grow from near stagnation to modern levels. Reductions in child mortality further induce substitution from child quantity to quality. This substitution explains the transition to both high income growth rates and lower fertility levels. Reduced child mortality is fundamental to the transition from low-growth to high-growth economies. It is another example of how economic growth and demography are intimately connected. Eventually, the transition from a rural agricultural society to an urban industrial economy involves a linkage in the shift from low income to high income and from high fertility to lower fertility.

The more sophisticated an economy, the greater the emphasis on an educated and skilled workforce. Parents then tend to devote more resources to each child as it becomes more economically rational to have fewer, but better educated, children. Across the world, improvements in education are associated with declines in fertility. The converse is that in societies where there is less economic development, there is little economic rationale to have fewer children. Economies that are dependent on low-skilled labour still retain higher fertility rates because the need for quantity outweighs the demand for quality. Notice the reinforcing trend. People experiencing lower levels of economic development, as in the case of countries in the global South that are often dependent on raw material supply to the global North, have less incentive to have fewer children. The higher levels of fertility in the global South compared to the global North are not the cause of uneven development but the result.

Second, the growing prohibition on child labour in the nineteenth and early twentieth centuries meant that children were no longer a source of income from employment, at least formal employment, so having more children did not necessarily increase household income. As the emphasis shifted to educating children, so the trend moved to having fewer rather than more children.

Third, urban economies provided more opportunities for paid work for women. Many of the early industrial factories, especially in textiles, employed large amounts of female labour. Women now had more opportunities outside the narrow and constricted realm of having children. During both the First World War and the Second World War, women were also employed in a range of jobs usually done by men. Figure 3.3, for example, shows women

Figure 3.3 Women at work in Busch Terminal, Brooklyn, USA, 1918
Source: National Archives and Records Administration, https://commons.wikimedia.org/wiki/File:86-G-6T-1-busch-works.tif.

at work in Industrial City in Brooklyn in 1918. This economic transformation involved a DT because one consequence of female participation in the formal workforce is a decline in the birth rate and family size. The combination of economic transformation and urbanization reinforced the transition towards lower fertility rates.

Urbanization has now levelled off in much of the global North. The bulk of urban growth is now occurring in the global South, with rural to urban migration still playing a major part. Although in some areas, such as South Asia, urban population growth is mainly driven by natural growth rather than rural to urban migration, in areas of very rapid urbanization, such as sub-Saharan Africa, younger children are less likely to die at a younger age in cities than in rural areas.

Biopolitics

It was the French theorist Michel Foucault who introduced the notion of biopolitics. It involves an enumeration, categorization and management of the population to maximize life potential and economic productivity. It imagines the people of the state as both a statistical and political object and human life as a central object of science and governance. Population data are generated to guide government policy. One useful definition of biopolitics is: "a field of politics concerning the administration and optimization of the vital attributes of life (fertility, mortality, quality …). Biopolitical governance or *biogovernance*, is aimed at the management of the vital characteristics of human populations and exercised in the name of optimizing individual and collective life, health and welfare" (Greenhalgh 2009: 208).

Biopolitics involves state power over our bodies. The state has the power to imprison people and, in some states, still has the political authority to execute people. Government decrees the age of sexual consent and when people can get married, go to school, retire with state benefits and a host of other important activities. To be sure, before the transition the state played an important role, but beginning in the nineteenth century the state became more actively involved in the range of activities that impacted demography. These include specifying the age when people can legally work, marry and have children. Today, government rules and regulations encase people's everyday decision about their life choices. More directly, the state is involved in public health. Indeed, the very idea of a sphere of "public health" emerged in the nineteenth century.

Government now plays a major and pervasive role in demography by making public policies that shape and guide birth rates, fertility levels and mortality rates. Government policies are used to – or at least try to, both directly and indirectly – raise or decrease the birth rate, improve life expectancy and reduce mortality. Demography is now an integral part of governance and governmentality. Biopolitics involves not only a statistical enumeration of the population but also a whole repertoire of agencies and suite of practices to shape human life.

The modern state was shaped by the emergence of a biopolitics while demographic trends were increasingly influenced by the form and nature of biopolitics. The state has played a major role in the demographic tradition by pursuing policies that reduced death rates and improved public health and by crafting policies that encouraged certain form of household formation. Biopolitics is now an essential form of power in the modern political era that in turn defines modern life.

SUMMARY

This chapter considered the context for the beginnings of the DT in the nineteenth century. We looked at the liminal period from 1800 to 1870 that marked the beginnings of a change from a population characterized by high fertility with the majority of women's lives dominated by having and rearing children. A time of patriarchal dominance, it was also a time of demographic commentary. Writing at a time of population growth and political upheaval, Thomas Malthus originated the idea that population growth tends to overwhelm the food supply. He believed that population increased at a geometric rate while food supply only increased at an arithmetic rate; so over time there would be more population than food available. Despite evidence to the contrary, his ideas continue to reverberate down through the years. A fuller evaluation of his legacy is presented in Chapter 8.

In fact, food supply did increase dramatically as part of major changes during this demographic pre-transition. The first agricultural revolution increased food supply and reduced the need for agricultural labour. Subsequent agricultural revolutions, such as the Green Revolution, which created high-yielding crop varieties and greater use of fertilizers and pesticides, have all increased agricultural productivity across the globe. Malthusian melancholy is largely unfounded.

The first and subsequent agricultural revolutions meant a decline in the demand for labour and allowed a shift from rural to urban populations. In cities, fertility levels are lower as there tends to be a substitution from child quantity to child quality. The combination of agricultural change and urbanization leads to smaller families with less children. The economic shift from agriculture to industry and services, as well as growing female labour participation rates, are also linked to the emphasis on fewer children.

The nineteenth century also saw the fuller emergence of a biopolitics that involved greater involvement by governments and the state to count and classify populations. Biopolitics also sought to influence demographic outcomes. In subsequent chapters we evaluate policies to boost and limit population growth.

The main takeaway is that the combination of changes in agriculture, economic structure, growing female labour participation rates and increased urbanization all resulted in a transition towards higher-growth economies and lower fertility rates. Demographic changes were both the cause and effect of the broader social and economic changes associated with agricultural revolutions, industrial revolutions and large-scale urbanization.

FURTHER READING

Malthus
Bashford, A. & J. Chaplin (eds) 2016. *The New Worlds of Thomas Robert Malthus*. Princeton, NJ: Princeton University Press.
Petersen, W. 2018. *Malthus: Founder of Modern Demography*. Abingdon: Routledge.
Smith, K. 2013. *The Malthusian Controversy*. Abingdon: Routledge.

Children and family
King, M. 2007. "Concepts of childhood: what we know and where we might go". *Renaissance Quarterly* 60: 371–407.

McInnes, J. & J. Diaz 2009. "The reproductive revolution". *Sociological Review* 57: 264–84.
Newman, S. 2017. "Infanticide". *Aeon*. https://aeon.co/essays/the-roots-of-infanticide-run-deep-and-begin-with-poverty.

Agricultural revolution
Bocquet-Appel, J. 2011. "The agricultural demographic transition during and after the agriculture inventions". *Current Anthropology* 52(S4): S497–S510.
Galor, O. 2012. "The demographic transition: causes and consequences". *Cliometrica* 6(1): 1–28.
Gage, T. & S. DeWitte 2009. "What do we know about the agricultural demographic transition?" *Current Anthropology* 50(5): 649–55.
Ingholt, M., L. Simonsen & M. van Wijhe 2022. "Agricultural revolution, demographic change, or medical modernization? The disappearance of malaria from Denmark". *Social Science & Medicine*. https://forskning.ruc.dk/en/publications/agricultural-revolution-demographic-change-or-medical-modernization.

Industrial revolution
Bar, M. & O. Leukhina 2010. "Demographic transition and industrial revolution: a macroeconomic investigation". *Review of Economic Dynamics* 13(2): 424–51.
Khan, A. 2008. "The industrial revolution and the demographic transition". *Business Review* 1: 9–15.
O'Rourke, K., A. Rahman & A. Taylor 2013. "Luddites, the industrial revolution, and the demographic transition". *Journal of Economic Growth* 18: 373–409.
Simon, J. 1994. "Demographic causes and consequences of the industrial revolution". *Journal of European Economic History* 23(1): 141.
Teitelbaum, M. 2014. *The British Fertility Decline: Demographic Transition in the Crucible of the Industrial Revolution*. Princeton, NJ: Princeton University Press.

Urbanization
Adams, J. 2022. "Urbanization, long-run growth, and the demographic transition". *Journal of Demographic Economics* 88(1): 31–77.
Becker, G. 2009. *Human Capital: A Theoretical and Empirical Analysis, with Special Reference to Education*. Chicago: University of Chicago Press.
Bocquier, R. 2015. "Which transition comes first? Urban and demographic transitions in Belgium and Sweden". *Demographic Research* 33: 1297–332.
Canning, D. 2011. "The causes and consequences of demographic transition". *Population Studies* 65(3): 353–61.
Dyson, T. 2011. "The role of the demographic transition in the process of urbanization". *Population and Development Review* 37: 34–54.
Jedwab, R., L. Christiaensen & M. Gindelsky 2017. "Demography, urbanization and development: rural push, urban pull and … urban push?" *Journal of Urban Economics* 98: 6–16.
Lee, R. 2015. "Becker and the demographic transition". *Journal of Demographic Economics* 81(1): 67–74.

Sato, Y. & K. Yamamoto 2005. "Population concentration, urbanization, and demographic transition". *Journal of Urban Economics* 58(1): 45–61.

World Bank 2021. "Demographic trends and urbanization". *The World Bank.* https://www.worldbank.org/en/topic/urbandevelopment/publication/demographic-trends-and-urbanization.

Biopolitics

Goerres, A. & P. Vanhuysse (eds) 2021. *Global Political Demography: The Politics of Population Change.* Cham, CH: Palgrave Macmillan.

Greenhalgh, S. & E. Winckler 2005. *Governing China's Population: From Leninist to Neoliberal Biopolitics.* Palo Alto, CA: Stanford University Press.

Macey, D. 2009. "Rethinking biopolitics, race and power in the wake of Foucault". *Theory, Culture & Society* 26(6): 186–205.

Mavelli, L. 2017. "Governing the resilience of neoliberalism through biopolitics". *European Journal of International Relations* 23(3): 489–512.

Palonen, E. 2021. "Democracy vs. demography: rethinking politics and the people as debate". *Thesis Eleven* 164(1): 88–103.

Purdy, J. 2006. "The new biopolitics: autonomy, demography, and nationhood". *BYU Law Review* 889–955.

Repo, J. 2016. "Gender equality as biopolitical governmentality in a neoliberal European Union". *Social Politics* 23(2): 307–28.

Teitelbaum, M. 2015. "Political demography: powerful trends under-attended by demographic science". *Population Studies* 69(1): S87–95.

4
The growing population

Look again at Figure 2.1, where you can see that stages 2 and 3 of the DT initially involve a rapid decline in death rates while birth rates remain high. Then, death rates decline as birth rates start to slow down. The two stages combined are associated with a rapid rise in total population. This occurred first in the global North, then, by the last half of the twentieth century, in the global South. In this chapter, we consider the dynamics and consequences of this expanding population.

DECLINING INFANT MORTALITY

A dramatic change resulted from the decline in infant and youth mortality. This is an important demographic variable because up until the mid-twentieth century, infant mortality rates were responsible for almost half of total mortality. Infant mortality measures those who died in their first year of life. Youth mortality measures those who died before reaching the age of 15. Throughout most of human history, almost half of newborns died in the first year of life, and for those that survived around 50 per cent died as youths. Today, the global infant mortality rate is 4.3 per cent and under 5 per cent for youth mortality. It is a staggering decrease and is a major reason for rapid population growth. Figure 4.1 depicts the rapid fall-off in rates in just one country, the UK.

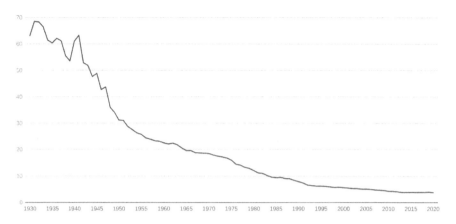

Figure 4.1 Infant mortality in the UK, 1930–2020
Source: Office for National Statistics, https://closer.ac.uk/wp-content/uploads/Infant-mortality-rate-graph-3.png.

There was a historical and geographical dimension to these fundamental demographic changes. The decline of child mortality occurred first in the global North in the late nineteenth and first half of the twentieth century, while it mainly took effect in the global South much later, in the final third of the twentieth century. Some statistics reveal these differences. Even as late as 1990, the child mortality rate in Burkina Faso was almost 19.8 per cent while it was only 1.2 per cent in the USA. But by 2017, Burkina Faso's rate was only 8.1 per cent and it was below 1 per cent in the USA

Newborn babies and youths are particularly vulnerable to a variety of diseases and ailments. But with adequate care and attention they can survive, and with improved survival rates the population can climb very quickly. The main reason behind the fall in infant mortality was the improvements in health and nutrition. We can look at just one example to stand in for many. As late as 1870, whooping cough killed approximately 1,300 per million children aged under the age of 15 in England and Wales. Also known as pertussis, it is a highly contagious respiratory disease and is particularly dangerous for infants. However, it can be avoided and cured by vaccines and antibiotics. The bacterium that causes the infection was discovered in 1906, a vaccine was first developed in the 1930s and fast-acting, effective antibiotics became available in the 1940s. The start of mass vaccination in the 1950s reduced the mortality rate to close to zero. By 1970, whooping cough had become a very minor, non-fatal childhood infection in the UK. Whooping cough is still fatal in parts of the global South, with approximately 50,000 deaths in 2020, but even this figure is a dramatic improvement from the 138,000 worldwide deaths in 1990.

Better maternal care, involving better professional care and attention for mothers, meant that having children became less dangerous and more mothers and newborns survived. The global figure for maternal mortality rate per 100,000 live births was approximately 335 in 1990. By 2023 it was reduced to fewer than 175. Maternal mortality remains a problem in certain areas, however, even in rich countries. In the USA, one study found that a significant number of maternal deaths, almost 80 per cent, were because of preventable causes (Trost *et al.* 2022). This study also found that the maternal death rate was distinctly higher for women of colour and indigenous woman. Compared to white women, they were three times more likely to die in childbirth. The main causes of maternal deaths include cardiac and coronary problems, overdose because of postpartum depression and haemorrhaging. Other causes were infection, embolism and disorders related to high blood pressure. The results reveal the deep roots of inequality in maternal health care.

The overall effect of improvements in nutrition and health care was the decline in child mortality from 40 per cent in 1800 to 27 per cent in 1950. By 2020, the global figure had fallen to 4.3 per cent. There are still pockets in the world where mortality rates remain high. In the Central African Republic, for example, one in ten infants die, compared to Iceland where just one in 1,000 infants die. There is a similar pattern in youth mortality; in Somalia the rate is 14.8 per cent while in Iceland it is 0.3 per cent. There are also differences between high-income countries. The USA has a child mortality rate 57 per cent higher than other high-income countries. The difference is because of the country's higher rates of deaths from traffic accidents and firearms, and a lack of a universal health coverage and limited social welfare, all factors that lead to much higher infant mortality, especially for lower-income households.

PEOPLE LIVING LONGER

Population growth was also fuelled by increased life expectancy, which kicked in after the decline in infant mortality. The improvements in nutrition and public health that reduced child mortality also had the effect of gradually raising life expectancy. Reducing child mortality is a relatively quick fix compared to lengthening life expectancy since adults embody the effects of deprivation, poor health and poverty over their lifetime. It thus takes much longer to lengthen life expectancy.

Life expectancy is the mean length of life. Life expectancy at birth is a measure of the mean length of life of those born in a specific year. Life expectancy has tended to increase across the globe. Before the beginning of the nineteenth century, no country had a life expectancy longer than 40 years. The world average was around 30. By 1950 it was around 46 and by 2023 had reached 73.

Economic development, especially in the global North, led to higher incomes, more food and better nutrition. There was also a health revolution that involved a better understanding of deadly diseases and a growing ability to counter their effects. There were and still are huge variations in life expectancy. In general, because of difference in national wealth and hence differences in health outcomes, there is still a 20-year difference between life expectancy in the global North and the global South. In 2021, the average life expectancy for Japan was 84.8, 80.7 for the UK and 77.2 for the USA. It is much lower in the global South where life expectancy is 62.7 for Uganda and 53.9 for the Democratic Republic of Congo. These global variations reflect differences in national wealth that feed into differences in levels of personal affluence, access to medical care and overall life experiences that all influence the average length of human life. This is highlighted by the differential impacts of disease and viruses around the world. Take the case of influenza. From 1900 to 1940 there was a decline in those dying from influenza. If you were born in 1940 you only had a third of the risk of dying compared to those born in 1900. And those born in 1980 had half the risk of those born in 1940. In the UK, the death ratio for those aged over 65 was 45 per 1,000 population. In the Democratic Republic of Congo, in contrast, the figure is 73.2.

RAPID POPULATION GROWTH

As more people live longer and fewer infants die, the population increases. Before a decline in birth rates, the result is rapid population growth, and even as birth rates continue to fall, population growth continues.

Rapid population growth occurred first in the global North. Take the case of the UK. In England the population almost doubled from 1851 to 1901, from 16.8 million to 30.5 million. In Scotland, over the same time, the increase was from 0.6 million to 2 million. The main reason was the declining mortality rate as birth rates remained high. The average fertility rate was 4.8 children per women in 1871. The birth rate did not drop below two (the replacement rate) until the mid-twentieth century.

Malthusian expansionism and settler colonialism

The rapid rise in population in the nineteenth and early twentieth century in the global North, in countries such as the UK, generated economic pressures as well as political uncertainty and anxiety. Population growth could run ahead of employment opportunities.

The rapid population growth of domestic populations was a major reason behind the nineteenth- and early twentieth-century settler colonialism, which we can define as the presence of a settler population in land previously occupied by indigenous peoples. Rapid population growth at home was a major reason behind the mass emigration to the "New World", especially to the lightly populated grasslands of the Americas, South Africa, Australia and New Zealand. The process involved the dispossession of indigenous populations, the establishment of settler colonies and their integration into the global economy by producing raw materials such as wheat and beef for metropolitan markets. It was a continent-wide phenomenon. Scandinavian settlers moved to the upper Midwest of the USA, British emigrants moved to Australia and New Zealand and families from the Italian peninsula emigrated to North and South America.

In some cases, such as the Irish famine of 1845–52, emigration became a way to avoid starvation and death. During these years, Ireland's population fell by 25 per cent as one million people died from starvation and hunger-related diseases and a further million emigrated, many of them to Australia, Britain and North America.

During an age of imperialism, with much of the global South coming under the control of neocolonial and colonial powers, it was possible to siphon off excess populations into newly appropriated land, especially the vast grasslands. It reduced pressure at home and helped in the more complete appropriation and control of territory abroad.

Settler colonialism was lubricated by government programmes in both sending and receiving countries. The governments of Argentina, Australia, Canada and the USA actively promoted immigration from Europe to settle and commodify the land, develop national economies and network them into global markets. A variety of private interests, including land development companies, shipping companies and railroad interests, were also involved. It took on a self-generating character of chain migration, as early settlers provided a bridgehead and information source for subsequent settlers. Settler colonialism involved promoting overseas emigration and the marginalization and sometimes eradiation of the indigenous populations. The lands were emptied rather than empty.

The term *Malthusian expansionism* was initially used with specific reference to Japanese migration-driven expansion in the early twentieth century (Lu 2019). As the Japanese population increased, several emigration schemes were launched. The *Japanese Striving Society* (*Nippon Rikko Kai*) was established in the early twentieth century to promote Japanese emigration in the hopes that landless farmers in Japan would become prosperous settlers in a variety of countries including Brazil and the USA, especially California and Texas. Later, attention shifted to Northeast Asia. The Japanese government, with enormous domestic support, sought to "export" a million households to Manchuria in a classic case of military appropriation and settler colonialism.

Malthusian expansionism was a worldwide phenomenon, and the result was a transformation of the world through settler colonialism.

Policy responses to rapid population growth

There was a distinct class dimension to rapid population growth in the nineteenth and the first part of the twentieth century. As mortality rates declined, the most pronounced rates of growth were among the poorer families. It was not just a general increase in population but an increase in those at the lower end of the socioeconomic hierarchy. Political elites became to believe that growth could overwhelm the ability of society to cope. It is important to remember this fact to understand that many of the debates of the time regarding ideas about population control and family planning were thus intimately connected to ideas about what to do about the "poor" and the "lower classes". Rapid population growth unsettled the established order, especially as the greatest growth was among those with the least stake in the existing order. As political demands increased for forms of social welfare funded by taxation, the rich began to fear that they were underwriting the costs of the increase in the "lower classes".

There were two interlinked responses. The first was the rise of eugenics, which is often associated with the work of Francis Galton (1822–1911). A relative of Charles Darwin, he was born into a wealthy family. He developed a whole range of social statistics and was part of an empirically driven biopolitics that first emerged in the nineteenth century and blossomed in the twentieth. Galton was interested in the role of heredity in shaping human character. In terms of the nature–nurture dichotomy, he firmly came down in favour of nature as the principal cause of human behaviour and achievement. In his 1869 book *Hereditary Genius*, he outlined the idea that you could improve the human stock by promoting the birth of people from gifted families. The corollary was preventing the less gifted from reproducing. The term *eugenics* literally means "good birth". There was both positive eugenics, encouraging the so-called superior people to have more children, as well as a negative eugenics that sought to prevent the genetically inferior from having children. Eugenics was pseudoscience. It took no account of the role of nurture, for example. The fact that the children of successful people tend to be successful is less a result of genetics than it is of being fortunate in being born into affluent families that can support and provide educational and career opportunities. It is your family wealth and post code as much your genetic code that tends to influence behavioural outcomes. Like many elite members of the time, Galton assumed that the rich and successful were rich and successful because they were hardworking and smart. The poor were poor because they were lazy and stupid. Eugenics legitimized vast social inequalities with the veneer of science.

As population increased, especially for the so-called poorer classes, there was a fear that the population would be overwhelmed by the so-called genetically inferior. In the USA, negative eugenics was actively promoted in the first half of the twentieth century when various states introduced the sterilization of criminals and the so-called mentally defective. Supreme Court Justice Oliver Wendell Holmes, in a 1927 ruling that upheld the state of Virginia's right to decide who could and could not have children, noted: "It is better for all the world, if instead of waiting to execute degenerate offspring for crime, or to let them starve for their imbecility, society can prevent those who are manifestly unfit from continuing their kind ... three generations of imbeciles are enough" (*Buck v. Bell* 1927).

Sterilization was also actively promoted in Nazi Germany, Switzerland and throughout Scandinavia. The Nazi regime took eugenics to a more extreme level, killing those considered mentally defective and promoting "breeding" programmes for Aryan-looking peoples. Under the Lebensborn project initiated by Heinrich Himmler in 1935 to boost the declining German population to 120 million, only "racially pure" men and women were encouraged to have more children.

A second and at times interlinked response was the rise of family-planning practices and programmes. We can consider the work of Margaret Sanger (1879–1966) as an exemplar. She was one of 11 children born into a large family of poor immigrant parents. She attributed her mother's death at the age of 50 to the physical toll of multiple pregnancies. In her early experience of nursing in the inner city, she became aware of the relationships between uncontrolled fertility, with high rates of infant and maternal mortality, and poverty. She was acutely aware of the negative consequences of unwanted pregnancies and illegal abortions from her nursing experience in the inner city. She strongly believed that the need to control family size and pregnancies was crucial to ending family poverty and promoting female emancipation. She was a feminist who worked all her life to promote family planning and easy access to contraception. She is often credited with developing the term "birth control". In 1912 she wrote a series of articles about birth control and sex education under the title *What Every Girl Should Know*. In 1916 she opened the first birth control clinic in the USA, in Brooklyn. She was indicted for mailing materials that advocated birth control and for distributing diaphragms. She served 30 days in jail, but her legal appeals finally led to the changes in federal law that subsequently allowed doctors to prescribe contraception for medical purposes. Legal actions against her and prison time did not stop her drive and determination. In 1921 she founded the American Birth Control League. In 1948 she became the first president of International Planned Parenthood and campaigned for birth control in countries around the world. With funding from a wealthy heiress, she recruited a researcher to produce the oral contraceptive known as the pill, which became one of the most widely used and easily available birth control measures.

At times her promotion of birth control and family planning intersected with the eugenics movement, especially with regard to preventing so-called unfit individuals from having children. However, she did resign from the American Birth Control League because of the eugenic leanings of some of its leaders, who had promoted contraception as a means of slowing birth rates among the poor. She is now sometimes charged with racism since she did focus her efforts on minority communities. But her principal aim was to empower women. Most Black women at the time tended to be poor and have limited access to health care, and were especially vulnerable to unplanned pregnancy. Her legacy is overwhelmingly positive in terms of family planning, but there is a tinge of the eugenic and racist assumptions that were standard at the time. At times she flirted with eugenics rhetoric, a very strong discourse at the time that was prevalent throughout the USA. Her critics point to these writings while her supporters tend to be more lenient, sometimes arguing that the eugenics movement was so powerful that she needed their assistance to promote birth control. She sometimes used the racist language of the time in some of her writings, but her main aim and abiding legacy was to empower all women to give them some autonomy over their bodies, and in doing so free them from a cycle of multiple pregnancies and enforced poverty. Her focus was on voluntary birth control and public health programmes. She believed that enforced motherhood, at a time when having multiple childbirths was more dangerous than it is now, denied a woman's right to life and liberty.

Margaret Sanger is an interesting exemplar because her life's work follows the trajectory of family planning in the twentieth century. At the beginning it was scarcely mentioned except by a few pioneers such as Sanger. In the misogynistic and sexist discourses of the time, family planning was not seen as a legitimate concern of public policy. There was widespread resistance to giving women the power to control both decisions. However, as the century progressed, the pioneering work of reformers such as Margaret Sanger managed to change the discourse. Family planning and contraception became more taken for granted in modern life. There was and sometimes still is considerable resistance from social conservatives and many religious hierarchies, especially in the Roman Catholic Church and among those that worried it was upsetting the traditional sexist order. But as family planning became more accepted and contraception methods became cheaper and more reliable, more women around the world began to use it. Even in deeply Catholic countries, contraception use increased. There are still battles about family planning, especially about the issue of abortion, but family planning and contraception is now an important part of our modern world. Birth control technology is accessible and relatively cheap. There are still areas of unmet demand, with costs and access varying across the world. But now family planning and contraception is widespread, common and accepted in most countries in the world, especially in the global North where contraception is widely used and is an important part of keeping birth rates low.

Population growth in the global South

The decline in birth rates was much slower to take hold in the global South, where birth rate remained higher and so population continued to increase. Today, countries with high growth rates include Niger (3.66 per cent per annum), Uganda (3.22) and Nigeria (2.53). In the case of Niger, the annual rate will lead to a doubling of the population in under 15 years. The population profile of Niger is shown in Figure 4.2. Note that the age cohorts are in two-year stages, The profile is pyramidal with a wide base of very young people narrowing quickly with age. Population growth rates are much lower for richer countries and in some cases growth rates are negative, such as Japan (−0.41) and Italy (−0.11). It is 0.49 for the UK and 0.68 for the USA, but most of this growth comes from immigration exceeding emigration.

Countries with very high birth rates tend to have much younger populations. Consider the case of Afghanistan. Although the birth rate has been steadily falling – from 7.45 births per woman in the 1960s to 4.18 in 2020 – it is still high. Child mortality has decreased from 180 per 1,000 in 1990 to 60.8 in 2020. High birth rates and declining mortality rates, especially for children,

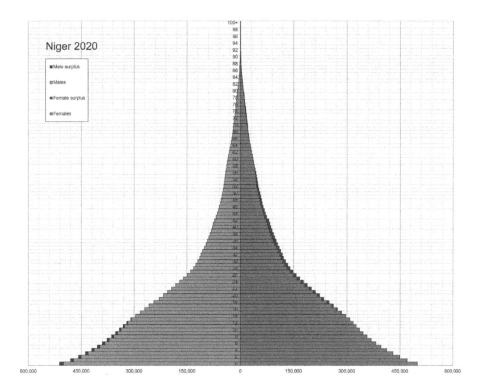

Figure 4.2 Population pyramid of Niger, 2020

Source: Generated from US Census Bureau International Database, https://commons.wikimedia.org/wiki/File:Niger_single_age_population_pyramid_2020.png. Licensed under the Creative Commons Attribution-Share Alike 4.0 International license.

means a rapid population increase. In 1990 the population of Afghanistan was 13.2 million. By 2020 it was estimated at close to 40 million: a tripling of the population inside 30 years. Such rapid population growth can overwhelm limited growth and employment opportunities. A rapid increase in population makes feeding all the people a major challenge and almost 23 million Afghans are severely hungry. Providing educational resources for a rapidly rising population is another major challenge even for middle-income countries, and especially for a low-income country such as Afghanistan. Creating employment and education for young people has challenged Afghani governments for the last 30 years. Many of the younger, more educated Afghans take the opportunity, where possible, to move abroad seeking a better life compared to the limited and diminishing opportunities at home. Behind the political fractures and recurring crises in the country, demographic challenges play a significant role. There are many reasons behind the current difficulties of Afghanistan, but incredibly rapid population growth in the context of a very low-income country beset by ethnic tension and religious rivalry is surely one of them.

The dependency ratio is defined as the ratio of the number of dependents to the total working-age population in a country. It is often calculated using the people aged under 15 and over 65 as the dependent population, while those aged 15–64 are considered to be the productive or working population. To be sure, these figures are just approximations of dependency since in much of the global South many children under the age of 15 work in both the formal and informal economies, while in both the global North and global South significant numbers of people aged over 65 continue to work. So it is an imperfect statistic but one that is commonly used. There are two variations. The youth dependency ratio is the population aged 0 to 14 divided by the population of working age, generally 15–64. The old-age dependency ratio is the population above 64 divided by the population age 15–64. In the earlier stages of the DT, the main characteristic is youth dependency. The top ten countries currently with the highest youth dependency ratio are all in Africa and include Niger (108), Mali (96) and Somalia (95). Afghanistan, with almost 42 per cent of its population aged below 15, has a dependency ratio of 80. In contrast the ratio is 27 for the UK, 28 for the USA and 20 for Japan.

For countries experiencing stages 2 and 3 of the DT, the high youth dependency ratio puts extra pressure on governments, especially those in poor countries. There are a large number of fiscal resources needed to educate and care for a relatively young population. Faced with explosive population growth and a high youth dependency ratio, many governments seek to limit birth rates as a matter of economic necessity.

FAMILY PLANNING IN THE GLOBAL SOUTH

In the 1960s and 1970s a dominant narrative was that population growth was major problem. Popular books such as *The Population Bomb*, first published in 1968, painted a bleak picture of rapid growth overwhelming society's ability to cope. The narrative was given legitimacy by a whole series of institutions and organizations that saw a desperate need for curbing population growth. Ideas and funds flowed from the intellectual and policy infrastructure of the global North to shape population policies for the global South. There was also an eager adoption by many governments in the global South fearful of having their development potential undercut by too rapid population growth. In 1952, India was the first country to formally adopt a policy of slowing population growth.

Family planning was promoted by a variety international non-governmental organization, such as the United Nations and the World Bank, as well as private organizations such as the Rockefeller and Ford Foundations. Large-scale family programmes were made possible because of new medical technologies such as diaphragms and safer condoms, and the cheapening cost of effective pharmaceutical contraception measures such as the pill. Despite these new developments, there was and still is an unmet demand: the discrepancy between women's stated preference for the number and timing of children and their actual contraceptive use. One goal of family-planning programmes was to reduce this unmet demand so that women who wanted contraception could get it.

Programmes focused on educating people about the benefits of smaller families and increasing accessibility to contraception. There were also more coercive methods. In 1976, India instituted a sterilization programme. A total of 22 million men were sterilized. The policy was not all that successful even on its own terms, since many of the men sterilized were older men who had achieved the desired family size and were participating for the benefits such as new washing machines. Households with more than two children were routinely denied access to educational grants, meal programmes and even the right to run for political office.

How effective were the programmes? Overall, the research shows that they increased the prevalence and use of contraception and played a part in reducing birth rates and in stemming population growth. It is difficult, however, to pull apart the independent effect of these family-planning programmes since reductions in fertility are also because of greater female participation in the labour force, rising affluence, better education and a whole host of factors connected to economic development and growth. Economic development and growth, it turns out, is the best cure for reducing high birth rates.

The programmes were criticized. One major criticism was that many of these programmes reduced women's autonomy, and in some countries, such as China and India, there were varying degrees of coercion. The emphasis was too often on controlling woman. Much of the emphasis and onus was placed on controlling women's bodies, sometimes coercively, in contrast to much less emphasis on things such as vasectomies for men. Other criticisms of the programmes included too narrow a focus on contraceptive technology, which in earlier years had more pronounced safety issues. However, most research found that family-planning programmes did reduce birth rates and maternal mortality and improved child health.

What was evident was the role of economic development that lifted people from poverty, especially rural poverty, and the growing emancipation of women from rigid patriarchal structures. There were also powerful demonstration effects. In Brazil, for example, studies have highlighted the important role of television shows, especially the telenovelas (soap operas) watched by millions of viewers that are especially popular with women. These shows were watched by many women across the country and what they saw were affluent, successful woman with small families. This provided a model for women across the country who saw women play roles other than being a permanent mother. One study, for example, found that decreases in fertility were stronger in the years immediately following telenovelas that portrayed messages of upward social mobility (La Ferrara *et al.* 2012). The influence of Brazil's popular television shows, and their depiction of women having small families, greater independence and more autonomy, all helped to reduce fertility rates as well as making divorce more common. By increasing awareness of many social issues, the television shows changed demographic patterns.

In India, total fertility rates began to fall in the 1960s and today the fertility rate stands below the world average of 2.5. The decline is in part because of improvements in economic conditions, but there was also the diffusion of the acceptance of family planning through the social hierarchy. In the earlier years, the decline in fertility was most marked among educated women, but by the 1990s two-thirds of India's fertility decline was among illiterate women using contraceptives. In this case, with limited socioeconomic advancement, the argument that contraception follows development and education is not so convincing. What was more important in this case was the role of social networks and mass media in providing more information about contraceptives and family planning. It is poor, uneducated women who are driving the fertility decline in India.

CASE STUDIES

For a more granular understanding, let's look at the implementation of family planning in selected countries. Policies to reduce birth rates took a number of different forms. The most dramatic was China's one-child policy.

China

The idea of curbing population growth was first mooted by the political leadership in China in 1953 when it approved a law on contraception and abortion. However, population decline in the wake of famine and political upheaval meant that the plan was abandoned. By the late 1970s, China's population was approaching the one billion mark. In 1949 China's population was 540 million. By 1979 it had increased to 969 million: almost a doubling of the population in 30 years. The Chinese leadership was worried that the rapid population growth would overwhelm the capacity of the country to cope.

A family-planning campaign began in 1971. The official theme was "one child isn't too few, two are just fine and three are too many". Another slogan used was "later, longer and fewer" to encourage women to marry later, have a longer period between the birth of the first and second child and to have only two children. The campaign was relatively successful and China's fertility rate halved between 1971 and 1978 and was already on the way down before the official one-child policy was announced (see Figure 4.3). In September 1980 the Chinese Communist Party formally introduced the one-child policy. It was initially meant to be countrywide but there was easier enforcement in urban areas, where there was a closer monitoring of residents. In effect, there was essentially a two-tier system with urban couples only allowed to have one child and rural couples able to have a second child, especially if the first child was female. But as China urbanized more people came under official scrutiny.

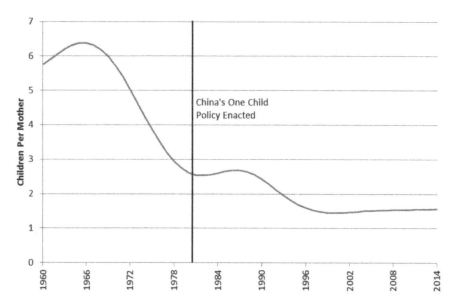

Figure 4.3 China's total fertility rate, 1960–2014
Source: https://braddlibby.wordpress.com/2011/07/07/
the-one-child-policys-effect-on-chinese-fertility/.

The policy involved making contraception methods widely available and offering financial incentives and preferential treatment, such as additional food rations to those who complied, while imposing sanctions and those who violated the policy. In 1980 the Communist Party ordered its 38 million members to have only one child. In 1982 birth control was enshrined as the duty of every Chinese citizen. At certain times, such as the late 1980s, there were more coercive measures such as forced abortions and sterilization. The state bureaucracy enforced birth control with the monitoring of local records on each woman of childbearing age.

Fertility rates fell from 5.9 births per woman in 1970 to around 1.6 by 2000, although we should add that China's fertility rate had dropped sharply before the enactment of the one-child policy. There were several unintended consequences over and above the policy objective of reducing population growth. The first was a skewing of the sex ratio. When restricted to having just one child, many households, especially in rural areas, decided to abort female foetuses. The introduction of cheap and effective sex determination such as ultrasound made it easier for people to identify the gender of the foetus. When given the choice, significant numbers decided to only ensure male foetuses through to birth. The result was more male children were born. There was an increase in the number of female children placed in orphanages or abandoned, and female children were adopted by families in the West, half of them in the USA. Today, China has 35 million more men than women. The country has a male to female ratio of 104 to 100. For the 15–19 age group the ratio in 2021 was 116 males to 100 females. The imbalance led to a sharp decline in the population simply because there were fewer females available for marriage and procreation.

A second consequence was changing family structure. A typical urban family with only one child leads, decades later, to one child responsible for four grandparents. With the limited social welfare, it is often children who are responsible for looking after their ageing parents and grandparents. The one-child policy meant the burden for looking after four grandparents fell on the narrow shoulders of just one grandchild.

Because of the policy, the birth of many children went unreported. Their undocumented status made it difficult to obtain education and employment, especially for those moving from rural areas to the city. As the policy effects unfolded, the number of people aged between 15 and 59 dropped nearly seven percentage points while those over 60 increased. China got older very quickly.

In 2014 the Chinese government eased the one-child policy, allowing couples to have two children if one of the spouses was a single child. The policy was finally abandoned in 2016, but by this time many of the newly formed Chinese urban middle class were aiming to have no more than two children. In 2021 the policy was relaxed to let parents have three children. But by then, China's fertility level fell below replacement, and by 2022 population growth turned into population decline.

A careful analysis of the policy suggests two conclusions. First, the family-planning campaigns of the 1970s were part of the forces that reduced China's fertility rate by half, although it has proved difficult to untangle the precise impact of the programme compared to, say, urbanization and an economic boom that led to the creation of a large urban middle class. Second, as Figure 4.3 reveals, China's fertility rate was already falling and would have declined substantially after 1978 even without the one-child policy. New economic opportunities reduced both the need and the desire for children and would have led to a drop in fertility levels even without the one-child policy. In other words, it seems that basic macroeconomic factors rather than the specific one-child policy were more responsible for the decline in fertility. As one careful analysis concluded: "Although the enforcement of the one child policy may have mildly accelerated the fertility transition in China, it also brought substantial costs, including political costs, human rights concerns, and more rapidly ageing population, and an imbalanced sex ratio resulting from a preference for sons. In retrospect, one may question need for introducing the one child policy in China" (Zhang 2017: 156).

Thailand

Thailand took a less coercive approach to reducing population growth. In 1970, the year the government began to address the issue, the growth rate was close to 3 per cent and the average family in Thailand had five children. Thailand then achieved a reproductive revolution. From 1970 to the late 1980s fertility rates were halved through a community-based, grassroots campaign to promote family-planning methods, including greater use of condoms and vasectomies. By 1984, two-thirds of Thai women reported using contraception. One influential figure was Mechai Viravaidya, who in 1974 founded the Population and Community Development Association to connect the fight against poverty with family planning. He toured the country promoting family planning, distributing contraceptives and even persuading Buddhist monks to bless the programme. The programme involved almost 350,000 teachers and 12,000 community leaders. Thailand's population growth rate fell from 3 per cent in 1974 to 0.6 per cent in 2005 as the average number of children per family fell from five to two. Figure 4.4 shows the drop on fertility rates below replacement and the slowing down of population growth.

There were many factors in Thailand's favour. Women have a relatively high status in the country so female autonomy in family planning is more respected than in many other countries. The dominant religion of Buddhism saw little threat in the adoption of family planning and in many cases Buddhist monks became advocates. At the same time, it was becoming more expensive for families to have children because of the rising cost of consumer goods and education. There was the shift from child quantity to child quality as more Thais moved to the city.

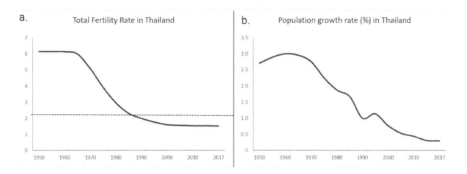

Figure 4.4 Fertility and growth rates in Thailand

Source: The Overpopulation Project, https://overpopulation-project.com/thailand-success-story-family-planning-with-creativity-and-humor/.

The Philippines

In 1970, Thailand and the Philippines had a similar population total of approximately 36 million. By 2022, Thailand's population was 70 million while the Philippines' was 118 million. The difference was in part because of the lack of family planning in the Philippines compared to Thailand.

As with many countries in the 1960s, population growth in the Philippines was considered a pressing issue and there were attempts at introducing family-planning measures. However, there was considerable resistance from Catholic bishops (the Philippines is a predominantly Catholic country) who were against the use of artificial methods of contraception. Population growth remained high, at 2.3 per cent, and fertility did not fall as rapidly as elsewhere because family-planning programmes were resisted by the Catholic hierarchy and influential conservatives. To placate the Catholic bishops, the Philippine government opted not to appropriate enough funds for contraception. There were other factors at work. The programmes that were introduced were deficient. There was limited access to contraception, not enough village supply points and few outreach workers, many of whom were lacked effective knowledge. The decline in fertility that did take place was achieved by economic development and rural to urban migration. More Filipino women decided to have fewer children. The fertility rate was 7.51 in 1950, 6.31 in 1970 and 3.8 in 2000. It was 2.7 in 2017 and by 2022 had fallen below the replacement rate of 1.9. However, the barriers to effective use of contraception continues and there is a considerable unmet need for family planning which is defined as sexually active women who want no more children or to delay having the next child. The quantity and quality of family-planning counselling at primary care clinics remains inadequate. The result is that one in four pregnancies are unintended and 600,000 unsafe abortions are performed each year.

Demography does have rippling effects. The basic demography of the Philippines – a marked increase in population at the same time as limited economic opportunity – was a significant factor in the large-scale emigration of Filipinos to find employment overseas. The Philippines effectively exported its excess population. There are over 12 million overseas Filipinos workers, almost 10 per cent of the national population, many of them young and female. While this transnational movement provides employment and income for families back home, it also comes at the significant personal cost of being far from home and family. Many Filipino children are raised by family members other than their birth mother, who work long hours overseas to give their children a better chance in life. There is also a national cost, as many of those who leave are hardworking, skilled and ambitious. The nation is drained of its human capital.

India

India was one of the first countries to adopt family planning in 1952. The Indian government sponsored family planning through making contraception more available. The result was dramatic as the fertility rate was halved from 5.7 in 1966 to 2.6 in 2009. The programme faced criticism because it targeted the poor more than the rich.

It is often difficult to tease out the independent effects of government policies because declines in fertility rates are also associated with economic growth and improvements in education for women. Indian states with the highest fertility rates have a lower literacy rate and lower socioeconomic growth. Most of the recent decline, from 4.0 in 1991 to 2.6 in 2004, occurred among uneducated women. And it was caused by a greater use of contraception.

Development is the best contraceptive. However, there is not a consistently robust relationship between socioeconomic change and fertility decline.

What seems just as persuasive is the diffusion of the acceptance of family planning and use of contraception. The two main channels are social networks and mass communication. The decline in states such as Andhra Pradesh occurred through the diffusion of information through friends and families, mass media and circuits of locally trusted experts such as doctors and nurses. There was also a spillover effect in which uneducated women were influenced by the fertility behaviour of educated women through social interactions, role models and mass media. There is also a long tradition of maids in rich households returning to rural areas with new social views. The fertility decline in India in recent years has been strongest among uneducated women, and several studies suggest that this is a diffusion process as new models of family size and spacing of childbirths take hold. Initially adopted by the richer, more educated households, these attitudes are diffusing through to poorer, uneducated families. Government policies may play a role in setting a policy, but the most effective measures diffuse through the population through social network, mass media and the adoption and acceptance of new practices of birth control.

Nigeria

Nigeria is the most populous country in Africa. Its demographic history followed a similar pattern to other low- and middle-income countries in the global South. A steep decline in infant mortality and very rapid population growth. The population of Nigeria grew from 45 million in 1960, at an annual rate of over 2 per cent, with a marked uptick to 3 per cent in 1980, to a population of 218.5 million by 2022.

What is interesting about Nigeria is the fact that the birth rate remains stubbornly high, at 5.3 births per women, one of the highest in the world. There are marked differences within the country more along religious-ethnic cleavages than class divisions. The predominantly Muslim Hausa/Fulani women in the North have a fertility rate of 8.0, while for the mainly Christian Igbo women it is 4.9 and 4.4 for the mixed Muslim-Christian Yoruba women. The Hausa/Fulani woman tend to have their first child before the age of 18 and childbearing increases with the number of years of childbearing exposure. Although there are certain differences in education levels, the main determinant of fertility difference is religion.

The federal government, faced with a very high youth dependency ratio and ballooning education expenses – spending on education is the largest recurrent expenditure for the Nigerian federal government – has sought to introduce various family-planning programmes. It has introduced two main population programmes. The first one in 1988, in collaboration with the World Bank, sought to reduce fertility from six children per family to four, set a marriage age at 18 and increase the spacing of childbirths. Funds were allocated to maternal-child health and education programmes. The programme met with fierce resistance in the Muslim north, where many who feel marginalized tend to resist the federal government's Western forms of education, especially for women. In 2004 a National Population Policy on Population for Sustainable Development was introduced. Again, it achieved very little as there was still opposition to family planning, which was especially strong in the north, a strong cultural preference for large families across the country, a lack of political will from political and religious leaders and a lack of funding. Since 2015, Nigeria has committed to train over 3,500 community health workers and to deliver a range of contraceptives, especially in rural areas. There are also attempts to promote the education of girls and increase the awareness of family-planning services. Yet Nigeria remains stuck in the earlier stages of the DT with persistently high although falling fertility rates. So, while infant mortality has decreased markedly and life expectancy is slowly inching up, fertility rates remain high. The population continues to grow, and the country has demographically locked in decades of future population growth.

There are regional differences to this national picture. In the northern part of the country, where Islam is dominant, large families are very common and desired by husbands as a show of wealth and success, polygamy is common, women marry very young and resistance to formal Western education, especially for females, is very high. Birth rates are lower in the south and among non-Muslims in part because of greater economic development. The Muslim north is poorer than the rest of the country. But across the country cultural capital accrues more to those with large families

Population numbers are also used in Nigeria to allocate resources from the federal government, so politicians, traditional rulers and religious leaders tend not to support population policies that limit the size of their constituencies. The economic preference for large families and the intense competition for resources between different ethnic and religious groups makes sustained family planning very difficult in Nigeria.

SUMMARY

In stages 2 and 3 of the DT there is a rapid fall in child mortality and a slightly slower increase in life expectancy. When birth rates far exceed mortality rates, the result is an increase in population. This occurred first in the global North and more recently in the global South.

Rapid population growth had several consequences. First, there was settler colonialism, involving migrants from Europe and Japan settling sparsely populated areas. Second, a variety of policies were initiated that ranged from eugenics to family-planning programmes. In the past 50 years considerable attention has been focused on controlling population growth in the global South. Policies ranged from the coercive to the more participatory. They are often associated with the marked decline in fertility rates, but it has proved difficult to separate out the effect of these policies from overall economic growth and increased female labour force participation. The policies ranged from the one-child policy in China to the successful and less coercive approach adopted by Thailand. In some countries, such as the Philippines, family-planning programmes were stymied by a lack of funding and opposition from the Catholic Church.

The main takeaway is that rapid population growth tests the resilience of societies. Responses can vary from encouraging emigration, suppressing birth rates (especially for the poor) and encouraging family-planning programmes. The greatest success occurs when there is easier access to contraception as well as economic development that raises living standards and new role models that valorize smaller families. In countries such as Nigeria, the decline of birth rates has stalled because of cultural preferences for larger families and religious affiliations. Rapid population growth can lead to a high youth dependency ratio that creates extra pressure to support the education and health of a relatively large number of young people relative to the working population.

FURTHER READING

Infant mortality
Volk, A. 2013. "Infant and child deaths". *Evolution and Human Behavior* 34: 182–91.

Malthusian colonialism
Lu, S. 2019. *The Making of Settler Colonialism*. Cambridge: Cambridge University Press.
Young, L. 1998. *Japan's Total Empire: Manchuria and the Culture of Wartime Imperialism*. Berkeley: University of California Press.

Family planning
Adebowale, A. 2019. "Ethnic disparities in fertility and its determinants in Nigeria". *Fertility Research and Practice* 5(3). https://doi.org/10.1186/s40738-019-0055-y.
Brahmanandam, N. & P. Arokiasamy 2017. "Fertility transition in Andhra Pradesh: role of diffusion in use of contraception among illiterate women". *Social Science Spectrum* 2(4): 239–47.
Chatterjee, N. & N. Riley 2001. "Planning an Indian modernity: the gendered politics of fertility control". *Signs: Journal of Women in Culture and Society* 26(3): 811–45.
Drèze, J. & M. Murthi 2001. "Fertility, education, and development: evidence from India". *Population and Development Review* 27(1): 33–63.
Herrin, A. 2007. "Development of the Philippines family planning programme: the early years 1967–80". In W. Robinson & J. Ross (eds), *The Global Family Planning Revolution: Three Decades of Population Policies and Programs*, 277–98. Washington, DC: World Bank.
Knodel, J. 1987. "Thailand's reproductive revolution". *Social Science* 72(1): 52–6.
La Ferrara, E., A. Chong & S. Duryea 2012. "Soap operas and fertility: evidence from Brazil". *American Economic Journal: Applied Economics* 4(4): 1–31.
Mydans, S. 2022. "'Captain Condom' turned the tide in Thailand's war on AIDS and overpopulation". *New York Times*. https://www.nytimes.com/2022/08/05/world/asia/thailand-aids-overpopulation-mechai.html.
Nagai, M. *et al.* 2019. "Opportunities lost: barriers to increasing the use of effective contraception in the Philippines". *PLoS ONE* 14(7). https://doi.org/10.1371/journal.pone.0218187.
Robinson, W. & J. Ross (eds) 2007. *The Global Family Planning Revolution: Three Decades of Population Policies and Programs*. Washington, DC: World Bank.
Seltzer, J. 2002. *The Origins and Evolution of Family Planning Programs in Developing Countries*. Santa Monica, CA: RAND.

5
The bulging population

We can see from Figure 1.1 that the rapid increase in population in stages 2 and 3 of the DT begins to lessen as fertility rates decline. The birth rate levels off and can even decline as women, for a variety of reasons, have fewer children. But the legacy of the population spurt continues to flow through the population pyramid, first as a youth bulge, then as an increase in the middle aged, and finally into a top-heavy, aged and ageing population. In this chapter we examine these different bulges, including the youth bulge and the gender bulge and the possibility of a demographic dividend.

THE YOUTH BULGE

Population surges work their way through the demographic pyramid to create distinct bulges. The rapid increase in births because of a decline in infant mortality creates a larger than average cohort. At first, it is a large cohort of babies that then ages into a large youth cohort. Take the case of Jamaica. In 2001, the country's largest ten-year cohort was aged 0–10. This created a high youth dependency ratio with a consequent drag on economic performance as resources had to be devoted to a largely non-productive population. By 2011 birth rates had fallen and the largest cohort was now 10–20, and then 20–30 in 2021 as the baby boom turned into a youth bulge.

The youth bulge is generally considered a larger than average cohort aged between 15 and 29. This is an age when many people are either still at home or just starting their independent lives. There has been a lot of theorizing about this youth bulge. Revolutions and major social upheavals tend to tend occur more often with large proportions of young, frustrated men. Young people tend to have more energy than older people, and they often have less commitment to the existing order, being less bound by tradition and often critical of their elders. They are the basic raw material of social revolution and political violence. The German sociologist Gunnar Heinsohn (2021) was perhaps the first to promote the notion that an excess of young people, especially young males, leads to a greater tendency for social unrest, war and terrorism. He suggested that the third and fourth sons often find it difficult to find prestigious positions in the existing hierarchies and are thus more open to joining revolutionary and destabilizing movements. Heinsohn claimed that most historical periods of social unrest can be explained because of the build-up of a youth bulge. He included European colonialism, twentieth-century fascism and ongoing conflicts today such as the Palestinian uprising and political terrorism.

When this bulge constitutes more than 15–20 per cent of the population, it has been linked to an increase in political instability and the possibility of increased political violence. This is not an iron rule, since it depends on the presence or absence of educational employment opportunities. Countries that do have a higher proportion of young males, such as Syria, Somalia, Afghanistan, South Sudan, Yemen and Egypt, do tend on average to have a more positive correlation with indices of conflict and instability. However, not all countries with similarly high male youth bulges – such as Bhutan, Botswana and Swaziland – have higher incidences of political violence. In countries with no youth bulge, such Denmark, Ireland, Canada, Japan and Spain, there are fewer incidents of political violence. However, these countries also have higher levels of development and national wealth. The key variables then are the level of economic development and access to economic opportunity.

Higher levels of crime are generally associated with young males. Worldwide, 90 per cent of all homicides are committed by male perpetrators. Most crimes are committed by people aged 15–24. Criminal activity slows or ceases as people age out of this cohort. There is a simple connection: as the percentage of the population aged 15–24 increases so does crime, and conversely when this cohort declines so does crime. This occurred in Canada and the United States in the 1990s and Brazil in the early 2000s. There is a fall-off in crime rates as the youth bulge declines in numbers and relative weight.

Several studies tested the argument that a youth bulge makes societies more susceptible to political violence. For the period 1950–2000, Henrik Urdal (2006) found that countries with particularly large youth bulges are three times more likely to experience serious armed conflict. These bulges provide greater opportunities for violence through the abundant supply of youth with low opportunity costs. The youth bulges led to an increase in both the opportunities and the motives for political violence. The interaction of youth bulges with economic decline and an expansion in higher education appears to increase the risk of terrorism. An educated young cohort without access to opportunity can be a destabilizing force in societies. In a more detailed study, Urdal and a colleague looked at 55 large urban centres in Asia and sub-Saharan Africa for the 1960–2006 period (Urdal & Hoelscher 2009). The male youth population bulge did not increase levels of social disorder. A more important factor was youth exclusion from economic opportunity, even in the absence of extraordinarily large urban youth population bulges. It is not simply the number of youth but their range of opportunity for active and meaningful participation in economic and political life that influences political conflict. This work is interesting because it is suggestive that it is not youth bulges on their own that make countries prone to conflict but the combination of youth bulges with few economic opportunities. Economic stagnation plays an important role in turning a youth bulge into a tinderbox of armed conflict. In some cases, migration may work as a safety valve for youth discontent.

Using data from 1998–2005 covering 127 countries, Alfred Marcus and colleagues found that youth bulges are correlated with violent conflict. They also showed that violence did fall off when the youth bulge was followed by a decline in the size of the youth cohort (Marcus *et al.* 2008). Evidence from sub-Saharan Africa suggested that a 1 per cent increase in the size of the population group aged 15–19 raises the risk of low-intensity conflict (Flueckiger & Ludwig 2018). But if we break down the type of political unrest then a more nuanced picture emerges. The youth bulge is more strongly linked to non-ethnic wars than to wars of ethnic conflict. The relative size of the youth bulge also matters in how corruption affects the internal stability of a political system. Using panel data covering the 1984–2012 period for more than 100 countries, Yair and Miodownik (2016) found that the effect of corruption on political stability depends on the youth bulge. Corruption is a more destabilizing factor for political systems when the share of the youth population in the adult population exceeds a critical level of approximately 20 per cent.

There is clearly a correlation between a youth bulge and social instability. Countries with more than 60 per cent of the population aged under 30 are at least four times more likely than countries with more mature populations to experience outbreaks of civil conflict. However, there is a difference between correlation and causation. Countries with a youth bulge also tend to be relatively poorer. The youth bulge is positively correlated with social conflict but its weight as an independent causal factor needs to be teased out.

We can look at the connection between youth bulges and social conflict in more detail through two examples: South Korea and the Arab Spring. Two political geographers, Gary Fuller and Forrest Pitts (1990), looked at the emergence of a youth bulge in South Korea in the 1970s and 1980s and its correlation with a rise in political unrest. At that time, South Korea was an authoritarian, undemocratic state ruled by a military junta. The expanding youth bulge was a significant source of resistance to military rule. Young people, workers and students regularly took to the streets to protest. One of the country's most prestigious universities, Seoul National University, was purposely located far from the centre of the city to minimize disruptive student protests. The 18-year rule of the military regime ended in 1979 after massive demonstrations took place across the country with young people in the vanguard. Political protest subsided after democracy was introduced and the youth bulge passed.

Second, there was a demographic context to the Arab Spring protests that swept across the Arab world in 2011. At the time, more than 60 per cent of the total population of the Middle East and North Africa (MENA) was less than 24 years of age and 30 per cent of the population was aged between 15 and 29, an unprecedented ratio of the young and very young to the total population. In Iraq, for example, the population aged 15–29 is approximately 91 per cent of the entire over-30 population. This youth bulge is the result of the high birth rates of the last two to three decades and the recent decline of birth rates. The median age in Libya is 24 and in Yemen it is 17. Compare this to the USA, where the median age is 37. In Egypt, 60 per cent of the total population are aged under 30 and 18 per cent are in the 17–25-year range. The youth bulge is clearly visible in the population pyramid of Egypt in 2020 shown in Figure 5.1. Across MENA, the proportion of 15–24-year-olds is 21 per cent of the total population and 34 per cent of the working-age population. The unemployment rate among this group is a very high 26 per cent. The Arab Spring had many causes, but a disenfranchised youth bulge was certainly a significant factor. Across the region this youth bulge is also associated with very high youth unemployment with an average of 31 per cent for youths aged 18–24 and greater than 36 per cent in Tunisia, Libya, Iraq and Oman.

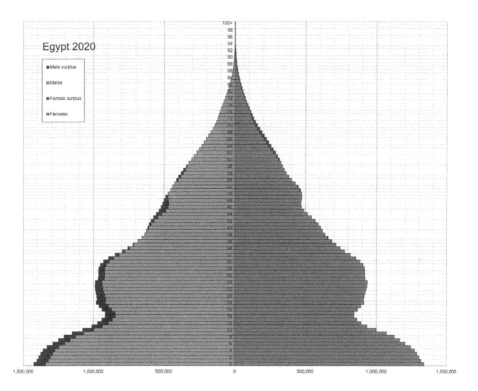

Figure 5.1 Population pyramid of Egypt, 2020

Source: Generated from US Census Bureau International Database, https://commons.wikimedia.org/wiki/File:Egypt_single_age_population_pyramid_2020.png. Licensed under the Creative Commons Attribution-Share Alike 4.0 International license.

In other regions of the world this youth bulge can turn into a demographic dividend as more people join the productive workforce. In MENA, by contrast, the bulge is associated with high unemployment and restricted employment opportunities. Youth across MENA countries currently have unemployment rates twice the world average. And in a twist from the situation in the USA and UK, where the better educated have lower unemployment, it is often the opposite in MENA where the educated youth have some of the highest unemployment rates as there are fewer opportunities in the national economies compared to the unskilled and less well educated. The result is a large mass of discontented, educated youth. Part of the demographics behind the Arab Spring, Islamic fundamentalism and the recruitment to militant groups is the discontent of this youth bulge unable to find employment or job opportunities commensurate with their education. Surveys reveal a high level of youth discontent as people respond that they feel there is no space for them in society as currently constituted. Young people across the region describe their state as one of "waithood" as they are unable to join the job market or establish a home, career and family of their own.

The youth bulge was a common reason given for the Arab Spring, but we should be careful in ascribing too much causation simply to the relative and absolute number of young people. Much of the commentary drew upon the work of the political scientist Samuel Huntington, whose influential 2011 book *The Clash of Civilizations and the Remaking of World Order* argued that the population explosion in Muslim countries is a significant feature of global politics. He saw a young Muslim population surge as leading to many small wars in Eurasia. The dominant narrative was that the MENA population is young with a high number of unemployed or underemployed and sclerotic economies that provide few opportunities for young people and young men in particular. The Arab Spring protests arose from a complex range of interlinked factors including inflation, corruption, lack of freedom, greater use of cell phones that allowed young people to keep in touch to organize demonstrations and, in some countries, higher levels of education. It was not just the level of unemployed youth but the large number of unemployed youths who had some education and access to the internet.

GENDER BULGES

There are not only differences between cohorts, with thick and thin cohorts of different sizes, there are also differences in terms of gender. If left to chance, the gender ratio is approximately evenly balanced at birth with roughly a ratio of 100 male births to 100 female births that carries on through the pyramid until the later stages. The ratio changes in the more elderly cohorts since women tend to live longer than men. Across the globe, the average life expectancy for women is 79. It is 72 for men. The respective numbers are 79/73 for the USA and 82/79 for the UK.

There are periods of dramatic change in the gender balance. Take the case of the First World War, when there were huge casualties among men. After this war there was a marked imbalance with more women than men. One study found that in regions with higher mortality rates, men were more likely to marry women of a higher social classes and were more likely to marry than women, out of wedlock births increased and divorce rates decreased (Abramitzky *et al.* 2011). The imbalanced ratio with more women than men meant that men improved their position in the marriage market, allowing them to marry up, had more possible marriage partners and were more able to find younger marriage partners. The politics of marriage and sexual relations are transformed when there is a distinct gender imbalance. In Russia after the Second World War, the high mortality rate among men meant that in the immediate postwar era there was a male scarcity, which led to lower rates of marriage and higher rates of non-marital births. Men had more bargaining power. There are also social implications of a weighted gender ratio. One study of family formation in the USA found that when there are fewer women than men, then men are more likely to be married and more sexually committed to a single partner (Schacht & Kramer 2016). The gender ratio shapes male behaviour towards women.

In many countries, especially in South and East Asia, there is a skewing of the population away from roughly gender parity towards having more males than females. With the introduction of more sophisticated technology, it is now easier to ascertain the gender of a foetus. It is also much cheaper, so the procedure is available to a wider range of people. In societies where there is a distinct bias towards having sons, the easy and quick recognition of the gender of a foetus can lead to early terminations of female foetuses. The result is a larger number of male births per female births. In the case of China, for example, there are now 121 male births for every 100 female births. It is 110 in South Korea and 108 in India. This trend is also occurring in fast-developing countries. In Vietnam, for example, the ratio of boys to girls at birth is now 114 to 100. Vietnam, like China, has a Confucian tradition that values sons above daughters since sons are a form of security for old age while daughters essentially are shipped off to their husbands' homes.

The gender disparity is particularly marked in China where the one-child policy meant that when families could decide the gender of their only child, many chose to see male foetuses through to birth but not females. Since 1964 the gender gap has been growing. There was close to parity in 1964, but it was 121 to 100 by 2020. The imbalance is evident in the population pyramid of China shown in Figure 5.2. Notice the excess male births for all cohorts,

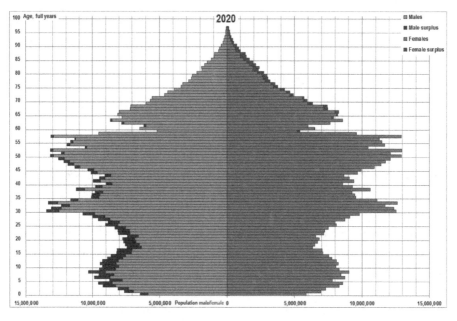

Figure 5.2 Population pyramid of China, 2020

Note: The graph represents population numbers by single-year age groups and sex on the date of the Census 2020.

Source: Wikipedia.org, https://en.wikipedia.org/wiki/Demographics_of_China#/media/File:China_population_sex_by_age_on_Nov,_1st,_2020.png. Reproduced under the CC BY-SA 4.0.

which is especially large for the more recent cohorts. In the cohorts aged over 65 there are more women than men because of differences greater male mortality. On average, women live longer than men.

One study showed that China's violent crime rate rose in tandem with the changing gender ratio (Edlund *et al.* 2013). Between 1988 and 2004, while other forms of crime such as corruption showed no increase, the violent crime rate increased. There was a positive correlation between the rising ratio of men to women and a higher crime rate. The general name for problems associated with this situation is the *bachelor bomb*. One study looked at six Asian countries and found that in regions with higher ratios of men to women there was greater self-reporting of sexual violence against women (Diamond-Smith & Rudolph 2018). There is empirical evidence that a rising number and proportion of unattached young men is associated with increased crime, higher rates of HIV and other sexually diseases and growing violence against women and girls. The exact connection between uneven sex ratios and increased violence has yet to be fully uncovered. It may be that, unable to find a female partner, heterosexual males and especially those with less resources and hence less ability to attract partners experience rising rates of frustration and anger that leads to a greater likelihood of misogynistic attitudes and behaviours.

Skewed sex ratios also influence consumer spending. Unmarried male consumers facing a shortage of women tend to purchase more expensive luxury vehicles than their married peers. The greatest degree of conspicuous consumption tends to occur, according to a survey in China, in regions where there are more males to females (Grier *et al.* 2016). In tight and competitive dating/marriage markets, men feel the need to show off to attract a mate.

Across a swath of territory from MENA through South Asia to China, more men are born than women. The complexity of the social and economic impacts is clear if we compare the two most populous countries in the world: China and India. Both have hypermasculine gender ratios. The marriage squeeze works out differently in the two countries. In China, bride prices have increased as women are in demand, while in India, men have had to settle for much smaller dowries. In both countries heterosexual men in rural areas with little opportunity to marry experience growing depression, loneliness and suicide. The proliferation of psychological issues among bachelors, especially poor rural-originating bachelors in urban areas, has led to an increase in violence against women and girls.

There is also the opposite to the bachelor bomb: the gender imbalance of more women than men. This is especially marked in countries such as Russia and former territories of the USSR where males constitute 45 per cent of the total population but males over 65 only 30 per cent. In the countries of the former Soviet Union only Tajikistan has more men than women, whereas across Russia, Estonia, Latvia, Lithuania, Belarus and Ukraine there are roughly 8.5 men to every ten women. Some of the reasons include heavy alcoholism rates among men that has reduced their life expectancy markedly. It is no accident then that there is a vigorous market in western Europe and North American for men looking for female partners in Russia and eastern Europe.

COHORTS LARGE AND SMALL, UNLUCKY AND LUCKY

There are also differences between cohorts. The economist Richard Easterlin suggested that the fortunes of individual members of a cohort depend in part on the size of that cohort relative to the size of the total population. It is luckier to be born in the relatively smaller cohort than a larger cohort since, holding everything else constant, there are likely to be more opportunities. For example, if you were born in the United States in the 1930s only 18.7 babies were born for every 1,000 people compared to 29.5 in 1915 and 24.1 in 1950. People tend to have more opportunities if they are born in a demographic trough than those born during demographic peaks. Total births per 1,000 varied from 30.1 in 1910 to a low of 18.7 in 1935. If you were born during the demographic trough from roughly 1930 to 1950, for example, you had a greater chance of scholarships.

There are also lucky and unlucky cohorts. A large-scale study of different age cohorts in China since 1949 found intense population-based competition in schooling and employment for large-size cohorts (Shu & Ye 2022). Cohort size was negatively associated with family income and happiness. The unluckiest cohort was born during the turmoil of the Cultural Revolution (1966–76).

A cohort that enters a job market during economic depressions suffers from what is termed *recession scarring*. One study in the USA found that recession-scarred graduates had lower earnings, lower socioeconomic status, poorer health and higher rates of mortality (Schwandt & von Wachter 2019).

Those without a college degree suffer even stronger income losses than college graduates. The negative impacts persist in the long run. College and high school graduates who graduate in a tough job market of a recession have less income than those who graduate in good years for at least 10–15 years. The longer-term impacts for the scarred cohorts include higher death rates when they reach middle age and more unhealthy behaviours such as smoking, drinking and eating poorly. Recession-scarred graduates had higher death rates in mid-life and experience more deaths of despair. The bad luck of looking for a job during hard times can often lead to higher rates of mortality, poorer health and lower income over both the short and the surprisingly longer term.

DEMOGRAPHIC DIVIDEND

In the DT model, the baby boom cohort turns into the youth bulge cohort that, as it ages through the years, become a large number of the economically active and productive. The demography dividend refers to the possible economic benefits of the increase in the size and relative weight of the population aged 15–64. There is a window of opportunity when birth rates have fallen, so the dependency ratio is low, but lengthening life expectancy has not yet increased the old-age dependency ratio. The dividend occurs in an economic sweet spot, a period when there is a more economically productive population and less very young and less very old. The size of the working-age population is a significant driver of economic growth as it can increase productivity, savings and investment. This demographic effect can exceed 6 per cent of gross domestic product (GDP) over three decades.

The dividend lies behind the enhanced growth rates of national economies at specific times. A demographic dividend swept across the global South, including East Asia, first in Japan in the 1960s, then South Korea and China, and more recently Vietnam, South Asia and South America, giving many national economies a significant boost. We can attribute, at least in part, the spectacular recent economic growth of countries from Japan and China to India and Brazil to the increasing size of the 15–64 cohort. The plateauing of this dividend generation is a significant feature of slowing economic growth rates in rapidly ageing Japan and more recently China.

The trajectory of Vietnam is typical for many low- and middle-income countries. In the 1980s, the population was increasing by one million every year. Today, the total population is around 97 million. Fertility rates have declined from five children per woman in 1979 to just over two by 2020. The result is a demographic dividend, with 67 per cent of the population now aged between 15 and 64. This potential dividend had the opportunity to turn into an actual dividend because the 1980s also saw a series of economic reforms, including privatization, deregulation and the enhancement of private land use rights that shifted the economy from being state-controlled to a more market-based system. In a three-month period in 2018, 26,000 new enterprises were established and foreign direct investment for the year reached almost US$4 billion. The simultaneity of the demographic dividend with a loosening of economic restrictions led to impressive economic growth. Between 2002 and 2018 more than 45 million, almost half the total population, were lifted out of poverty. Not all benefited. Ethnic minorities, especially those that lived in the countryside, fared less well.

There are also differences within the high-income countries. Due to higher birth rates and higher immigration, the USA has a higher proportion of the working-age population than comparably rich countries such as France and Japan. And this is one reason for the fact that from 1990 to 2022, growth in real GDP was around 110 per cent for the USA and only 60 per cent for France and less than 30 per cent in Japan. This has not led to corresponding improvements in the quality of life for ordinary Americans compared to the French and Japanese because most of the economic gains in the USA have accrued to the wealthiest. Comparing the USA with France and Japan regarding life expectancy tells a different picture from overall growth rates. Respectively, the figures are 77.2, 82.1 and 84.6. This is a reminder that the demographic dividend may increase national wealth, but an important feature is how this wealth is distributed. Not all benefit equally from the dividend.

In theory, a population age structure in which there are significantly larger cohorts in the economically active ages of 15–64 tends to promote economic growth. With fewer dependents that are either very young or very old, more capital can be invested in job-creating schemes. The enlarged tax base provides extra government resources since, with fewer outgoings for the very young and the very old, more can be devoted to improving communication, upgrading infrastructure and direct capital investments. A demographic dividend has the possibility to create a virtuous cycle, with extra investment leading to more jobs that in turn promote further economic growth. But to realize the demographic dividend a country must provide the opportunities for the cohort to be productive. It is necessary therefore to improve education, infrastructure and health care and to promote good governance and other factors that facilitate the growth of human capital and turn the potential dividend into an actuality.

The demographic dividend needs to be carefully managed for the working-age population bulge to become a dividend rather than a problem. It requires investments in public health and education for its youth to acquire the skills for a competitive global market and the adoption of macroeconomic policies that ensure the optimal use of human resources. The possibilities, however, are enormous. In 2020 the average Indian will be only 29 years old in contrast to China's 37 years and Japan's 48.

The demographic dividend has the possibility of a large and growing labour force, but in order for this population to deliver growth and prosperity full participation is needed. Brazil's demographic dividend, for example, was substantially reduced by the fact that 70 per cent of the population was excluded from the consumer market through lack of resources and access to credit. And where there is gender discrimination, only half of the cohort has full participation. It is vital to increase labour force participation and enhance human productivity by investing in education, health, training and skill improvements. When females are given less opportunity the full advantages of the dividend are lost. Greater encouragement of female labour force participation can be achieved through legislation that encourages female participation, such as anti-gender bias programmes, as well as providing more autonomy to women regarding when and how many children they bear. An increase in skilled female labour can contribute significantly to economic growth during the DT.

We can consider opportunities for the demographic dividend if we take the case of the experience of girls and young women. The demographic dividend will be missed if child marriage is not prohibited and there is little encouragement to go to school, leading to a life of repeat pregnancies and maternal morbidity. If denied full entry into the formal sector, then a greater reliance on informal work can lead to greater insecurity and an insecure old age. On the other hand, the demographic dividend will be enhanced if these young women can go to school, find employment, have an adult marriage or relationship with healthy children and experience lifelong learning with an ability to have a secure old age. These are the perfect conditions for the demographic dividend to become a reality.

Some countries have actively promoted the transformation of human capital to maximize the demographic dividend. Take the case of Bangladesh. The fertility rate for women was 6.7 births in 1960, which dropped to 4.5 in 1990 and then fell again sharply to 2.0 by 2020. The previous baby boom turned into a demographic dividend. The dependency ratio began to go in Bangladesh's favour after 1980 when only 10 per cent were in the dividend cohorts, but by 2020 most of the population were of working age. The size of the dividend cohorts is evident in Figure 5.3. Notice the male surplus in the early cohorts and the female surplus in the older cohorts.

Bangladesh's dividend is likely to last until 2040. By that time, the population will have aged out. In 2020 almost 67 per cent of the population was aged between 15 and 64, almost 100 million people out of a total population of 170 million. This plentiful supply of labour has supported Bangladesh's industrialization, especially in the garment industry. In 2008, Bangladesh established a programme known as Vision 2021 with an emphasis on infrastructure development, technology innovation and human resource development. A key theme was the connecting of citizens to global digital markets. Bangladesh is already the second largest supplier of online labour after India and the IT sector is set to replace the garment industry as the country's biggest export earner. There are significant challenges to this goal, including lack of digital infrastructure, irregular power supply, workforce training and encouragement for digital freelancers. These drawbacks reduce the country's ability to become an IT player in the global market. The challenges are especially marked since youth unemployment has been increasing over the last decade, doubling from 6.4 per cent in 2010 to over 12 per cent by 2020. To achieve its ambitious goals, Bangladesh needs to upgrade infrastructure, fund education and school-based training, enhance the modernization of payment system support for e-commerce and giver greater encouragement to entrepreneurship. The country needs to overcome these challenges otherwise the demographic dividend could turn into a demographic disaster.

The window of opportunity for the demographic dividend does not stay open forever. It generally lasts anywhere between 20 and 40 years. If we use the figure of the under-15 population dropping below 30 per cent of the total

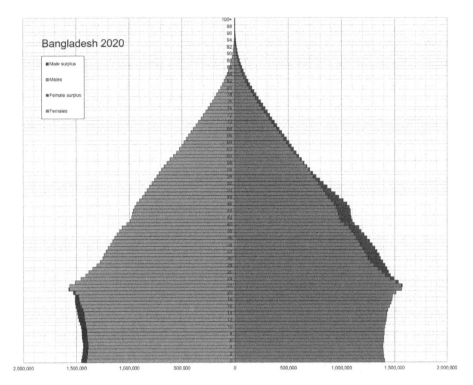

Figure 5.3 Population pyramid of Bangladesh, 2020

Source: Generated from US Census Bureau International Database, https://commons.wikimedia.org/wiki/File:Bangladesh_single_age_population_pyramid_2020.png. Licensed under the Creative Commons Attribution-Share Alike 4.0 International license.

population, while the 65 and older population is less than 15 per cent, then we can identify the different windows for different countries. A favourable dependency ratio only lasted in Japan from the mid-1960s to the mid-1990s and in the case of South Korea from the mid-1980s to 2020. A few countries still have significant time left in their window of opportunity. Indonesia's window is from the mid-2000s to 2040. For India it is from 2010 to 2050 and for the Philippines from, roughly, 2015 to 2050. China's dividend window, which began to open in 1990, is already beginning to close.

For economies built on cheap labour, the demographic dividend begins to change at the so-called Lewis turning point. Named after economist William

Arthur Lewis, the point is when the supply of cheap labour runs out. The increased demand for labour pushes up wages and economies lose their cheap labour cost advantage. China's spectacular growth from 1980 to 2010 was in part a function of the high proportion of working-age citizens between 20 and 65 years of age. However, the population aged quickly, especially with fewer children being born because of the one-child policy. China's decades of rapid economic growth built on a demographic dividend is coming to an end.

The dividend peaked in East Asia in 2010, and will peak in South Asia around 2040 and in sub-Saharan Africa in 2070. The future wave of demographic dividend population is shifting to Africa. Across sub-Saharan Africa, fertility rates are falling after decades of sustained growth, and so the baby bulge will age into the more economically productive years. With an increasing proportion of the economically active, Africa is well placed to build on this dividend for decades to come to create sustained economic development. This demographic windfall can provide an exceptional opportunity. Some estimates suggest that the demographic dividend could account for anywhere between 11 and 15 per cent of GDP growth by 2030, lead to a reduction in poverty for 50–60 million people and expand economic activity by 22 per cent (Ahmed *et al.* 2016). However, this is potential economic growth. Turning it into an actual dividend is dependent on whether governments and institutions can respond with effective policies.

SUMMARY

The population is not evenly divided between different age cohorts. Some are bigger than others while some are luckier than others. This chapter looked at some of the reasons for, and consequences of, these variations. Some are luckier, in terms of timing, in so far as they come onto dynamic job markets, whereas recession-scarred cohorts carry on the negative impacts into middle and old age. When you are born can sometimes be as important as where you are born. There is always the overriding effect of your family background, but the timing of your birth plays an important part. Demography may not be destiny but, in the case of cohort timing, it is an important if often little recognized part of life chances and social outcomes.

There are also variations in size. The movement through the DT creates population bulges as the baby boom of the early stages of the transition ages. First, there is the baby bulge, when there are significant numbers of very young children that place pressure on societies to generate enough economic growth to support this essentially economic unproductive cohort. It is then followed by a youth bulge, when there is a significantly large population aged between 15 and 29. This bulge is sometimes associated with political instability and rising crime rates. However, for a youth bulge to turn into a source of instability requires a number of other factors, such as suppressed economic growth, lack of access to employment and cultural marginalization. It is not just the number of youths but their level of integration into the economic and political mainstream. The youth bulge becomes a problem if it is denied full access to economic opportunities and political opportunities.

As the youth bulge ages it can turn into the demographic dividend, generally referred to as the increase in the size and relative weight of the population aged 15–64. This is generally considered the most economically active population, and so when the national population becomes dominated by this cohort, the opportunities for growth are magnified since there is less drag from high ratios for youth dependency and old-age dependency. Numerous studies have found that the greater the size of the 15–64 age group, the greater possibility of increases in gross capital formation and labour productivity. We can see very recent economic history – in the rise of the Asian economies and the rapid growth of countries such as Brazil and India – as being largely a result of demographic dividends.

The window of opportunity of the demographic dividend does not last forever. It first emerges as the birth rates decline but begins to close with an ageing population. Brazil's window was essentially the 1980s/1990s to 2025, and by 2030 its demographic profile will start to look like Japan's in the 2020s.

The demographic dividend arises from the rapid growth of the productive population relative to the consuming population. To enhance the golden opportunity of the demographic dividend requires family-planning programmes, child health investments, laws and policies against gender violence and discrimination, incentives to save, a strong social safety net and opportunities for lifelong learning. The demographic dividend is a window of opportunity not a given. It only becomes a reality with more investment in human capital, greater inclusivity and the right kinds of educational, health and labour market policies.

A gender bulge occurs when there is a substantial difference in male and female birth rates. This has occurred in the past because of the effects of war that tended to result in fewer marriageable men than women. More recently there is a distinct male bias because of the practice of aborting female foetuses. The downside of this disparity is sometimes referred to as the bachelor bomb and is associated with increased crime and violence against women. The changing gender ratio also impacts the relative bargaining power of men and women in the dating and marriage marketplace.

The main takeaway are that cohorts vary in size and fortune with significant social and economic impacts. These impacts are not mechanically produced but mediated, and hence they are exaggerated or minimized through social structures and by public policies. A youth bulge can be a source of dynamism and innovation and not necessarily a source of political unrest and violence. The demographic dividend is an opportunity that can be utilized as well as squandered. Demography is very important but it is not an independent source of destiny.

FURTHER READING

The youth bulge
Apolte, T. & L. Gerling 2018. "Youth bulges, insurrections and labor-market restrictions". *Public Choice* 175(1/2): 63–93.
Farzanegan, M. & S. Witthuhn 2017. "Corruption and political stability: does the youth bulge matter?" *European Journal of Political Economy* 49: 47–70.
Ganie, M. 2020. "Youth bulge and conflict". In O. P. Richmond and G. Visoka (eds), *Palgrave Encyclopedia of Peace and Conflict Studies*. London: Palgrave Macmillan.
Inayatullah, S. 2016. "Youth bulge: demographic dividend, time bomb, and other futures". *Journal of Futures Studies* 21(2): 21–34.
Massoud, T., J. Doces & C. Magee 2019. "Protests and the Arab Spring: an empirical investigation". *Polity* 51: 429–65.
Nordås, R. & C. Davenport 2013. "Fight the youth: youth bulges and state repression". *American Journal of Political Science* 57: 926–40.
Urdal, H. 2006. "A clash of generations? Youth bulges and political violence". *International Studies Quarterly* 50(3): 607–29.

Urdal, H. & K. Hoelscher 2009. "Urban youth bulges and social disorder: an empirical study of Asian and Sub-Saharan African cities". World Bank Policy Research Working Paper 5110.

Weber, H. 2019. "Age structure and political violence: a re-assessment of the 'youth bulge' hypothesis". *International Interactions* 45: 80–112.

Cohort differences

Brainerd, E. 2017. "The lasting effect of sex ratio imbalance on marriage and family: evidence from World War II in Russia". *Review of Economics & Statistics* 99(2): 229–42.

Guraine, J. 2022. "Recession scarring of college graduates entering labor market during a downturn". North Carolina Commerce Department. https://www.commerce.nc.gov/blog/2022/09/29/recession-scarring-college-graduates-entering-labor-market-during-downturn.

Schwandt, H. & T. von Wachter 2019. "Unlucky cohorts: estimating the long-term effects of entering the labor market in a recession in large cross-sectional data sets". *Journal of Labor Economics* 37(S1): S161–198.

Shu, X. & Y. Ye 2022. "Misfortune of children of the Cultural Revolution: cohort size, historical times, and life chances in China". In Y. Li & Y. Bian (eds), *Social Inequality in China*, 131–55. Singapore: World Scientific.

Gender imbalances

Diamond-Smith, N. & K. Rudolph 2018. "The association between uneven sex ratios and violence: evidence from 6 Asian countries". *PLoS ONE* 13(5): 1–10.

Jaffri, A. & R. Sadiq 2019. "Impact of gender imbalance on current account balance of Pakistan: an empirical analysis". *Pakistan Journal of Social Sciences* 39(3): 1187–95.

Griskevicius, V. *et al.* 2012. "The financial consequences of too many men: sex ratio effects on saving, borrowing, and spending". *Journal of Personality and Social Psychology* 102(1): 69.

Schacht, R. & K. Kramer 2016. "Patterns of family formation in response to sex ratio variation". *PLoS ONE* 11(8): 1–14.

Som, K. & R. Mishra 2014. "Gender imbalance: trends, pattern and its impact on West Bengal". *International Journal of Scientific and Research Publications* 4(7): 1–10.

Demographic dividend

Ahmad, M. & R. Khan 2019. "Does demographic transition with human capital dynamics matter for economic growth? A dynamic panel data approach to GMM". *Social Indicators Research* 142: 753–72.

Franco-Henao, L. *et al.* 2018. "The demographic transition in the Democratic Republic of Congo: facts and challenges to reach a demographic dividend". *African Population Studies* 32(2): 4273–90.

Haider, A. 2019. "Demographic dividend could turn into a demographic disaster". *Daily Star*. https://www.thedailystar.net/lifestyle/perspective/news/demographic-dividend-could-turn-demographic-disaster-1709272.

Lee, R. & A. Mason 2006. "What is the demographic dividend?". *Finance & Development: A Quarterly Magazine of the IMF* 17: 16–17.

Rahman, E., E. D'Silva & S. Peteranderl (eds) 2021. *The Demographic Dividend and the Power of Youth*. London: Anthem.

Singh, P. & S. Kumar 2021. "Demographic dividend in the age of neoliberal capitalism: an analysis of employment and employability in India". *Indian Journal of Labour Economics* 64(3): 595–619.

Striessnig, E. 2019. "The demographic metabolism model of human capital formation". In A. Bucci, K. Prettner & A. Prskawetz (eds), *Human Capital and Economic Growth*, 139–65. Cham, CH: Palgrave Macmillan.

6

The shrinking population

In stages 4 and 5 of the DT, birth rates fall further and average life expectancy extends. The baby boom of previous generations has moved through the demographic dividend and become an older population. This shift poses both new opportunities and challenges for all societies but especially those that do not have a strong social safety net. The richer countries have more resources to cope with a greying population.

FALLING BIRTH RATES

The total fertility rate (TFR) is defined as the average number of children born to each woman. It is also more commonly known as the birth rate. The population is stable with a birth rate of 2.1, which is considered the replacement rate. Higher than this leads to population growth, lower means population decline.

One of the most significant and globally widespread demographic changes is the decline of birth rates. Figure 6.1 shows the global trend. The birth rate has been dropping for the past 70 years. In 1963 the global birth rate was 5.3 births per women. By 2020 it had fallen to 2.3 births per woman and by 2050 it is estimated to drop to 2.1, approximately replacement level. At that stage population growth will stabilize. Of course, there is tremendous variation across the globe. There are still significantly regions with high birth rates. In 2020, in

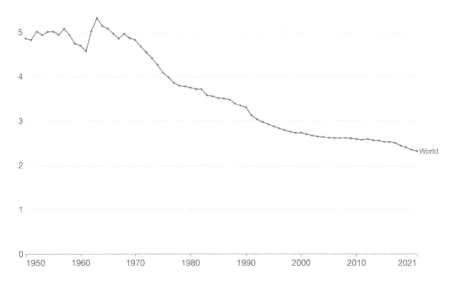

Figure 6.1 Global fertility rate

Source: Roser (2014). Reproduced under the CC BY 4.0 DEED licence https://creativecommons.org/licenses/by/4.0/.

Notes: The TFR is the number of children that would be born to a woman if she were to live to the end of her childbearing years and give birth to children at the current age-specific fertility rates.

Nigeria, Somalia and Chad, for example, there were over six births per woman. The figure for Niger was eight, making it the country with a highest percentage, almost 57 per cent, of its total population aged under 18.

In many other regions the birth rate has plummeted below replacement level. There are now at least 72 countries where the birth rate is below 2.1, whereas there were none in 1950. South Korea has the lowest birth rate at 0.78. Countries below the replacement level include Bangladesh (2.0), Sri Lanka (2.0), Vietnam (1.9), El Salvador (1.8), Brazil (1.6), the United Sates (1.64), the UK (1.56), Japan (1.34) and Italy (1.24).

This declining fertility is the main reason behind the slowing down of population growth and, in association with increased life expectancy, the greying of the population. The main reasons behind this staggering decline in fertility include lower infant mortality rates, which means women tend to have fewer babies, changing attitudes about the role of women, greater access to contraception and more women devoting more of their time and energy to education and work. For an example of fertility changes in a rich country, let us consider the USA.

In the USA, birth rates fell throughout the twentieth century. In 1900 the average rate was four children per women. It fell to just over two by 1980 and then held steady through to 2007. But then, as evident in Figure 6.2, there was a dramatic decline as the fertility rate declined from 2.1 in 2007 to around 1.6 by 2021 with a 20 per cent drop in births. Women were having children later in life. In 2021, the average age of women giving birth for the first time was 27.3 years of age. There were slight differences by ethnicity, with Asian women giving birth at an average age of 31.2 and Black mothers at 25.5. A survey by Pew Research found that woman with more education had fewer children. On average, those with a bachelor's degree had 1.7 children while those without a high school diploma had 2.9 children.

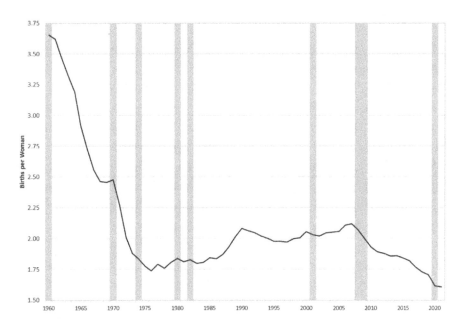

Figure 6.2 US fertility rate, 1960–2021

Source: Federal Reserve Bank of St Louis. https://www.stlouisfed.org/on-the-economy/2021/november/pandemic-influence-us-fertility-rates.

Note: Shading marks the year that sustained the recent recession (2020) and previous years that recorded at least six months in recession.

The decline in birth rates is not restricted to women delaying having children. More women are having fewer children over their entire childbearing years. The decline is widespread across different demographic groups, including Hispanic women, white non-Hispanic women and Black women. The largest declines in fertility are among those with a four-year college degree and those without a high school degree. The fertility rate for women with a high school degree but not a four-year degree has remained stable since 2007.

Women in the USA are having fewer births at all ages compared to previous cohorts. Births fluctuate according to economic conditions. They increase when the economy is strong and decrease when it is weaker. Figure 6.2 highlights years of economic recession. There was a drop in birth rates in the USA after the recessions of early 1980s, 1991 and 2008. However, there were also broader social trends at work. Kearney and Levine (2022) tried to tease out some of the reasons behind the marked fall since 2007. They looked at four economic factors: aggregate unemployment rate, generosity of welfare benefits, state minimum wage and expenditures, and child support enforcement. They also looked at certain reproductive health policies: abortion restrictions, health insurance coverage, mandatory coverage of country contraception, mandatory sex education and mandatory contraception instructional laws. They found that these factors combined only accounted for 6 per cent of the total decline. Their combined effect on declining birth rates was relatively small. Other factors, including costs of contraception, rent and childcare, also played little part. Neither did improving work conditions for women, rising student debt and declining religious observance. Their results suggest that attitudinal change was behind most of the decline. Women coming into their reproductive years in the twenty-first century are more likely to have been socialized into views of women having life pursuits outside the traditional roles of wives and mothers. The proportion of women reporting that work was as important as family rose from one-third to roughly one-half in surveys conducted in 2005 and in 2020. Women in the USA are having fewer children than previous cohorts, not because of fluctuating economic conditions, although that does play a part, but more because of a shift in attitudes and behaviours about the role of women and a growing sense that having more children is a burden as much as a blessing.

Americans are marrying later and thus compressing fertile years for conception. The medium age for a first marriage has increased. In the 1960s it was

23 years of age for men and 20 for women. By 2016, it was 30 for men and 28 for woman.

Behind the fall in birth rates is the increasing cost of childcare, housing and health care. It is difficult for the average US household with children to have only one breadwinner. To survive, most households need multiple people to be in work. The decline in average living standards for individual workers was masked by more people in a single household becoming wage earners. The stereotypical father at work and mother at home is no longer able to sustain a middle-class lifestyle for the average family. Many working mothers face a double burden of work, both outside the home and domestic labour in the home, especially the unpaid work of child rearing and childcare. Despite growing gender equality, mothers more than fathers carry a greater burden of household chores and caregiving. With the increase in the cost of childcare, women are making the understandable choice to either have fewer children or not to have children at all.

Many of the reasons for the decline of births in the USA extend across the globe. In both rich and poor countries, female labour participation has been growing and many families require multiple wage earners to sustain their lives. In these circumstances fertility levels decline.

The birth rate can also be influenced by deteriorating economic conditions. The economic crisis experienced by Greece in 2009 led to a decline in births. One study found that, in 2013, there were 20 per cent fewer births in Greek hospitals compared to the year before the economic crisis (Farfaras *et al.* 2016). Economic difficulties, as well as cuts in state spending because of the implementation of a strict austerity programme, had a significant impact on Greek families. One response was to increase contraceptive use to reduce the possibility of children. Overall, the net effect was a decrease in the birth rate.

In general, economic uncertainty leads to an increase in the age at first birth, a greater interbirth interval, the postponement of having children, greater use of contraception and ultimately a lower birth rate. Easier access to contraception and changes in attitude have given women more choice over when and whether to have children and how many to have. With the rising costs of childcare, growing domestic burdens for working mothers and the easing of restrictions on female labour participation, more women can imagine themselves having fewer children (perhaps none at all) and a larger life outside the domestic sphere.

DEALING WITH DECLINE

If birth rates decline below the replacement level of 2.1 then, assuming no immigration, population loss is the inevitable result. Nation states tend to worry if their population declines. It is a worry of long standing as this quote from the Bible attests: "In the multitude of people is the king's honour; but in the want of people is the destruction of the prince" (Proverbs 14:28).

Slowing growth and declining populations may be considered a good thing in terms of having the consequence of a lower human footprint, but there are two problems for national governments. The first is that a declining population is associated with an ageing population. As a population ages there is a changing ratio of taxpayers to recipients of social welfare programmes and contributors. Since most of the contributors are of working age, their declining numbers means that there are fewer people contributing to funds drawn on by a growing number of recipients. We explore this issue further in Chapter 7.

The second issue is the maintenance of economic growth. A decline in population, especially of the higher-spending working-age population, can lead to economic stagnation since there is a decline in investment spending as there is less demand. With a fall in population, the labour supply shrinks and the rate of capital formation declines. Perhaps the best example of this is Japan. The country's population peaked in the mid-1990s and ever since has struggled with a shrinking population and a stagnating economy, despite maintaining very low interest rates. Employment and growth can be maintained with deficit spending, but this leads to higher levels of public debt.

Most economic models suggest a relationship between the size of the economy and the size of the workforce. With fewer workers entering the labour force and older workers retiring, the workforce will shrink and GDP per capita will be reduced. With a larger workforce, more resources can be devoted to innovation. More new ideas arise and productivity increases. A declining population tends to reduce innovation and productivity. There are solutions to a declining working-age population. Governments could increase and encourage the immigration of working-age populations from other countries, especially through targeted immigration. This was a policy used extensively in the past in Europe and North America. We consider this option and its consequences in Chapter 8. Another response is to improve the productivity and efficiency of the smaller numbers of the working-age population. That requires major investments in education and training. A declining population raises all kinds of issues and problems in finding appropriate, affordable and politically feasible policy solutions.

China is a fascinating example of a rapid shift from population growth to population decline. In 2022, 9.56 million people were born in China. That is a significant number of new people ushered into the world. However, in the same year 10.41 million people died, and for the first time in six decades deaths in China outnumbered births. The number of births has been declining for about a decade. The year 2022 was an inflexion turning point marking a change in China's demographic trajectory from one of rapid population growth to slowing growth to absolute decline. Population growth has declined 94 per cent from eight million in 2011 to just under half a million in 2021. The working population, those aged 15–64, is estimated to decline from 579 million to 378 million by 2100. Currently every 100 working-age workers support 20 retirees, by 2100 every 100 workers will have to support 120 retirees.

The shift is in large part the result of previous economic success because as people have become wealthier, they live longer and have fewer children. The result is increasing life expectancy, declining birth rates, slowing population growth and an ageing population. The working-age population in China aged 15–59 made up 74 per cent of the population in 2010 but fell to 61 per cent in 2023 (different countries have differing definitions of working age: in China it is 15–59, in the USA it is generally defined as 15–64 and it is 16–64 for the UK). China's spectacular economic growth since 1990, which fuelled in large part the demographic dividend, is now being replaced by the difficulties of a declining working population and an increasing elderly population. By 2035 over 400 million people, almost a third of the entire population, are expected to be over 60. The result could be an increase in the cost of labour that may jeopardize China's global competitiveness and lead to labour shortages and declines in tax revenue. There will be fewer contributors to pension systems just as the number of retirees explodes.

The decline in the working-age population means a reduction in aggregate demand in the economy. China's population decline may curb national economic growth and consumption potential. The elderly in China currently limit their consumption and so a greying population will have less economic growth potential for the country. This demographic downturn may lessen China's ability to achieve its stated goal to replace its reliance on global exports with enhanced domestic demand. As China's global competitiveness is declining so is its ability to stimulate economic growth through domestic consumption.

There are some possibilities, however, of maintaining economic growth. The government can increase the retirement age, which is currently 50 years of age for women and 55 for men. The large number of agricultural workers, currently 23 per cent of the nation's total, is a large pool of labour that could be transferred to more productive non-agricultural sectors. There is also the floating population of rural migrants to the city who are not fully integrated into the formal economy. Domestic growth that fully utilizes this large pool of agricultural and informal labour could increase consumption levels by 30 per cent. And an ageing population could stimulate new forms of economic activity such as the growth of services related to elder care, health and ageing. The shrinking economic workforce could also stimulate greater use of automation and the development of robotics. China could also encourage greater immigration, especially of people of working age. However, China tends to be a net exporter rather than importer of people.

The fate of China's economy has global significance since it is such a large importer of raw materials from around the world and a major exporter of manufactured goods. China's rapid growth has stimulated the export receipts of primary producers around the world, from Australia to Zambia, while providing the global market with cheap consumer goods that reduce the cost of living. So, a slowing down of China's economic growth has global implications: less exports for primary producers and more expensive goods for importing nations. The demographic changes may be reducing the role of China as the major engine of global economic growth, a role it has played for the last 25 years. Indirectly, it may also generate internal dissent. The Chinese Communist Party (CCP) has maintained support and legitimacy because of economic growth. Over the past 30 years, a new middle class of approximately 200–500 million people has emerged from the economic transformation. The CCP has maintained legitimacy through its ability to maintain economic growth, expand national wealth, lift millions out of poverty and produce an expanded middle class. New aspirations have been created that can lead to disappointment if not realized. A Chinese political leadership whose legitimacy and continued support is tied to the benefits of economic growth and rising affluence will face rising discontent if incomes fail to rise and there is a fall in the standard of living after decades of growth. The reaction of the urban middle class in 2022 to the severity of pandemic restrictions gave us a brief glimpse of a large sector of the Chinese population that is unwilling to accept government restrictions. The social unrest, while relatively brief, did give an indication that there was a growing undercurrent of criticism of a tightly controlled centralized political system. Criticisms will be further fuelled by a slowdown in economic growth.

China is precariously balanced at perhaps the peak of its power, as the decades to follow may see slowing economic growth as the population declines. The working population will begin to shrink, perhaps reversing decades of economic growth. Superpowers are not only dangerous when they are expanding but they are equally, if not more, dangerous when they perceive a sense of decline. The demographic reality is that the Chinese national population will shrink and the working population will shrink even more. The demographic dividend and its positive economic implications have passed. China is now in the later stages of the DT and its first demographic dividend is at an end, with a future ageing, shrinking population and the sense that its demographic heyday is in the past. Superpowers may be more dangerous on their downward slide. The more muscular foreign policy and militarism of contemporary China under President Xi may thus be a response to a sense of possible decline.

In the second half of the twentieth century, China's population increased dramatically, with its population more than doubling. Concerns about overpopulation as a break on development meant that Chinese officials introduced coercive restrictions. The one-child policy was enforced from 1980 to 2015. It not only reduced the birth rate but also changed conceptions of family size. A smaller family size for many households became part of their move into the middle class as they could spend more on consumption and educating individual children. Education is a prime route for social mobility and having fewer children meant more investment in one child. This fundamental restructuring of ideas about family size are now firmly embedded in China. The YuWa Population Research Institute, a Beijing think tank, found that Chinese people's desire to have children was one of the lowest in the world, and to boost childbearing it is essential to reduce the burden of having children. For many women in China, having a baby means it is difficult to progress in their career, reduces household disposable income and creates an onerous double burden for many working mothers. As one Beijing woman told a reporter, "the working environment is really unfriendly to mothers" (Jett 2023).

BOOSTING BIRTH RATES

A shrinking of a nation's population is often worrisome for political elites and a sign and symbol of national decline. Population, after all, is the literal embodiment of the state. Fewer bodies equals a smaller state, smaller economy, smaller military and a smaller pool of human assets to promote economic growth, project military power and maintain international competitiveness. Fewer people means a possible reduction in the power of the state. One common response is trying to reverse the decline through pronatalist policies. The ability to boost the population ultimately rests on increasing the birth rate. It involves encouraging or forcing women to have more children. Pronatalist polices are a common feature of many societies. Policies can range from the nudge to the forceful push and from the suggestive to the compulsory. The more authoritarian the government the greater the likelihood of the compulsory push. The more democratic the nation, the stronger the suggestive nudge. Let us consider some examples of attempts to boost birth rates.

There is a long history of governments responding to low marriage and birth rates with techniques to boost birth rates and population size. From 1541 to 1871, birth rates in England declined because of the relatively late age at first marriage and the large numbers of people who never married. The average woman in England did not marry until 26 and the average man at 28. The age of first marriage only began to fall after 1750. Up to a quarter of the population never married. The English government, involved in a geopolitical with war with France, introduced the Marriage Duty Act in 1695 to encourage marriage and boost births. The legislation taxed bachelors over the age of 25 and childless widowers. There was also a cultural promotion of marriage and childbearing. The archetype of the old maid – a never married woman – took on disparaging tones. On the other side of the Channel, England's traditional enemy, France, focused on increasing births. Tens of thousands of midwives were trained to improve delivery techniques and to increase children's rate of survival.

The USSR, and later Russia, has had recurring issues of population decline because of falling birth rate. The bloody experience of the First World War, a civil war and the Second World War created huge death tolls and a massive loss of population. It is against this background that pronatalist polices were shaped. However, the USSR was also one of the first countries to legalize abortion. In 1920 the government legalized the procedure and provided relatively easy, cheap and sometimes free access. Abortions were easier to obtain, especially in urban areas. This created a recurring tension since access to easier abortions gave Russian women more reproductive choices. Soviet and later Russian demographic policy was shaped, on the one hand, by the recurring need to boost birth rates, and on the other hand by the reality of women's easy access to abortion. The state was always up against women's autonomy. The Soviet birth rate declined because, as more women left the rural areas for the cities to work, they had fewer children and easier access to abortion providers. In 1900, the fertility rate for Russia was 7.39 per woman during their reproductive years. By 1935 it had nearly halved to 4.49.

The Soviet leadership had initially believed that the improved living conditions and promised social plenty of the socialist utopia would allow women to have more children. It was a patriarchal notion that assumed women wanted to have children and only poverty and insecurity kept them from having more. In 1936, faced with the reality of the declining birth rate limiting the population growth necessary to ensure large militaries and pools of labour, the Soviet government banned abortion, a ban that lasted from 1936 to 1955. There were also financial incentives for Soviet women to carry more children to term and subsidies were given to mothers of seven or more children, who were also awarded the Medal of Maternal Glory. The policy was less concerned with female reproductive health and more about increasing manpower. The financial incentives soon disappeared, and many women continued to have (now illegal) abortions. In effect, women resisted the pressure to keep having children. In July 1944, the USSR launched more pronatalist policies against the background of huge population loses in the Second World War when 27 million Soviet soldiers and civilians died. The ratio of men to women of reproductive age fell to 19:100 in some rural areas. By 1945 the fertility rate had declined to 2.58. New laws were proposed to increase the postwar birth rate and provide a stronger demographic base for economic development. The legislation envisaged families as "the core institution of Soviet society". It included better health care for women and financial aid, and made it harder for married couples to get divorced. The Motherhood Medal programme provided subsidies to single mothers. The fertility rate rebounded briefly but only to 2.86 in 1950. The subsidies to mothers effectively ended in 1948. Abortion was made legal again by the post-Stalinist regime in 1955 and thereafter the fertility rate declined steadily to 1.25 in 2000.

By 2011, the Russian population had fallen to 138 million from 148 million in 1991. There was rising government concern about the declining birth rate slipping below replacement rate. In 2008 a new award, the Order of Parental Glory, was first given to parents of more than seven children along with US$825 when the seventh child reached three years of age. In 2010, the Russian government offered the equivalent of US$9,000 in cash to have a second child. There was an uptick in fertility to 1.82 in 2020 when the population increased to 143 million. Despite the increase in births, caused as much by improved economic conditions more than the pronatalist policies, the political elite still saw a problem. The demographic issues were entwined with a sense of Russian geopolitical decline since the fall of the Soviet Empire. Reduced geopolitical influence combined with a birth rate below replacement encouraged a pessimistic sense of decline and shrinkage. A new round of pronatalist policies was enacted. Putin, long worried about the implications of a declining population for a great power, recreated the Stalinist medal award when he announced in 2022 that the title of Mother Heroine would be awarded to women who have ten children. It came with a one-time payment of $16,500 if all the children survived and when the tenth child turned one year of age. Yet the ability of even an authoritarian government is limited. The culture of abortion is embedded in Russia. Abortion rates are declining but this is in part because of greater access to contraception. Women make their reproductive choices more according to wider socioeconomic conditions than government proclamations and inadequate fiscal incentives. The birth rate remained low even as people spent more on cars, so it was not a lack of money. Many Russian mothers feel that the social infrastructure for raising children is inadequate, and Russia does not offer child deductions on income tax returns. Even authoritarian governments have a hard time resisting the power of women to decide about having children, how many and when.

Under the communist dictatorship of Nicolae Ceaușescu, from 1974 to 1989, Romania experienced a transformation from an agrarian to an industrial-agrarian country. There was a decline in population as birth rates fell. To boost the population, he prohibited abortions, which were then freely available. The aim was to boost the population, not by encouraging people to have children but by stopping women having abortions. It was all stick and no carrot. With no improvements in childcare, Romanian families were forced to have more children and most experienced a marked decline in income. The policy was a fiasco and led to higher rates of infant mortality and at the extreme end more child abandonment. Ultimately, more than 100,000 children had to be institutionalized. The poor conditions for many of these children only came to light after the fall of the regime.

The birth rate in the Islamic Republic of Iran of is now 1.8, down from 2.5 in 2010. Iran used to promote birth control as a way to staunch very rapid population growth. Under more liberal administrations, such as the Rafsanjani presidency (1989–97), various family-planning measures were introduced, including encouraging the use of condoms, subsidizing vasectomies and laxer enforcement of laws restricting abortion. Now, under more theocratic administrations worried at the decline of the birth rate below replacement rate, condoms and vasectomies are no longer free. The government is trying to abolish access to abortions and contraception. Currently there are 400,000 abortions per year. The government is trying to register every woman in the early stages of pregnancy to make abortion even more difficult. There are also incentives to have larger families. Professors with larger families, for example, gain promotion easier. The government has pushed for maternity leave to be extended to nine months but faces pushback from employers. Zero interest loans are available to young people having children. One unintended consequence is an increase in young girls being forced to marry so that their husbands can cash in on the programme. Supreme Leader Khamenei describes not having children as a "decadent bourgeois affectation". But in Iran as elsewhere, the decision not to have children or to have fewer children is not an affectation but primarily an economic decision made by women and their families in a society burdened with high unemployment and the rising costs of having and caring for children.

Even governments that recently pursued policies to reduce birth rates are now changing to policies to boost them. Nowhere was the 180-degree shift in government policy so apparent as in China. After years of trying to reduce birth rates, the government, now faced with low birth rates and population decline, has turned to boosting birth rates. Policies include making infertility treatment more available to married women by including reproductive technology in the country's national medical system, expanding access to childcare services, reducing the cost of attending nursery school and working with employers to make offices more "family friendly". In 2016, the CCP altered its policy to allow married couples to have two children. In 2021, a three-child policy was inaugurated that encouraged couples to have three children.

The government is also trying to discourage abortions; China has among the highest rates of abortion globally. From 2015 to 2019, out of 40.2 million pregnancies annually, 17.7 million ended in abortion. About 78 per cent of unintended pregnancies in China end in abortion, compared with the global average of unintended pregnancies that end in abortion at 61 per cent. A significant reason is the cultural prioritization given to having male children. Foetuses identified as female are more likely to be aborted than those identified as male.

Authorities at the provincial and local levels have also tried to encourage the birth rate. Jiangsu province subsidizes companies to support female employees during their second and third periods of maternity leave. Companies are also reimbursed between 50–80 per cent of the social insurance paid to women who have a second or third child to counter discrimination against hiring women with children. Yunnan province offers one-time cash subsidies for families with second and third children.

Despite the recent adoption of these pronatalist policies, birth rates continue to decline. China's fertility rate has been below replacement levels since 1991. By 2022 it had fallen to 1.18 children per woman and the population is declining from a peak of 1.42 billion in 2021 to an estimated of fewer than 500–800 million by the end of the twenty-first century. Attempts to boost birth rates have come across the resistance of Chinese women who, like women elsewhere around the world, are concerned about the mounting costs of children's education, long working hours and low wages. It is a theme that is repeated across the globe. Families and women make their choices less on meagre cash handouts and more on childcare and living costs. The one-child policy also means that many young couples are often responsible for ageing parents and grandparents, so they already have heavy family responsibilities. It is expensive to raise a child and find family accommodation and good schools. More young Chinese are embracing what is referred to as a "double income no kids lifestyle", and fewer people are getting married and having children. In 2021 there were only 7.6 million marriages, the lowest since 1986, and those getting married for the first time dropped to a record low of 11.5 million people, the lowest since 1985.

For a growing number of countries – at least 27 in Europe and 18 in Asia – increasing the birth rate is now a stated national goal. To encourage a higher birth rate, pronatalist policies can either raise income for families with children or reduce the costs of having and raising children. Hungarian mothers with three or more children are eligible to receive a fixed monthly payment until the youngest child is eight years old. Part of the very low birth rates in counties such as Japan and South Korea is that women find it difficult to re-enter the workforce after having children, so they tend not to get married, and if they do they not to have children or only have one.

Many higher-income countries have introduced policies that provide child allowances or subsidies to women who give birth or to families with children. The province of Quebec paid families a newborn allowance that ranged from C$3,000 for a first child to C$8,000 for a third child. However, policies that directly subsidize the birth of a child lead to only a modest increase in fertility. A new, universal child benefit in Spain in 2007, for example, which gave parents a payment of about US$3,900, led to only a 6 per cent increase in the number of annual births. Others are more generous with free or subsidized childcare or paid family leave.

Research shows that women's ability to combine career and family with child rearing is a key determinant of fertility in high-income countries. Countries that make it easier for women to combine work and child rearing have both higher female participation rates and higher fertility rates. However, even with incentives, the TFR in almost all the richer countries has yet to move above two.

There are also implicit pronatalist policies that are often embedded into the tax structures of many countries. Traditionally, US tax policy, for example, favoured married couples with children. Married couples can reduce their tax-filing fees and can lower their tax burden by filing a joint tax return. Couples with children can reduce their taxes more than couples without children. As the share of married Americans continues to fall (it was down to 45 per cent in 2022), tax policies have distributional consequences. The tax system favours the "married couples with children" family model. More recent polices are more cognizant of the range of family forms, with the American Rescue Plan increasing the Child Tax Credit from $2,000 per child to $3,000 per child for children over the age of six and from $2,000 to $3,600 for single parents as well as for two-parent families.

As discussed earlier in this chapter, some pronatalist polices revolve around limiting access to abortion. It is estimated that the recent US Supreme Court decision in 2022 to overturn the *Roe v Wade* ruling, which gave abortion rights to women, will result in 100,000 fewer abortions per year. This is significant but not enough to raise the birth rate above replacement level.

The more effective pronatalist polices in high-income countries seem to be those that enable mothers to combine both work and child rearing. But even these are limited in their effectiveness. In Japan, for example, total government spending on families nearly quadrupled from 0.36 per cent of GDP in 1990–91 to 1.31 per cent in 2015. The pronatalist polices included expansions in child-care provision, paid family leave and child tax credits. The country's TFR still remains below 1.5. Policies that help parents to balance work and family, such as subsidized childcare or paid parental leave, are more effective pronatalist policies. Without that opportunity, women tend not to have children, whether they are married or unmarried. But even these more effective policies have limited the ability to boost birth rates. The pronatalist policies that have been implemented and evaluated in high-income countries are unlikely to lead to substantial or sustained increases in the birth rate. Olivetti and Petrongolo (2017) find that spending on early childhood education and childcare has the biggest effect on birth rates. For the USA, however, even one extra percentage point of GDP spent on these programmes would lead to an increase of only 0.3 more children per woman, an increase in the fertility from 1.66 to 1.69 but still far below replacement level.

Birth rates in the second demographic transition

The second DT is marked by below replacement fertility. Once a country reaches a certain level of economic development, fertility levels tend to fall. As more women are involved in the formal economy, it become more difficult to have more than one or two children. Many households require two people to work outside the home. Stopping work for one parent to have and raise your child can have deleterious economic effects. There is also an emphasis on child quality rather than child quantity. Having children in a competitive, more atomistic society with less access to grandparents and extended families places emotional and financial burdens on families. The result is that women tend to have less children.

The standard economic models of fertility behaviour assume that as people get richer, they invest more in children's quality of life and have fewer rather than more children. This seems to be borne out by empirical results. When women are in formal employment, having and raising children becomes more expensive since they are losing the opportunity to make money outside the home. However, several studies have also shown that most women in high-income countries aspire to have a family and a career. More mothers work in countries where favourable social norms and more flexible labour markets make it easier to combine a career and child rearing.

RIPPLING EFFECTS

Lower birth rates, like all demographic events, have rippling effects. Take the case of the USA, where birth rates remained roughly steady from 1970 to 2007 thereafter the fertility rate declined. There were 4.3 million births in 2007 but only 3.7 million in 2021. There are consequences for the education system in the country. The number of students graduating from high schools will begin a precipitous decline. Classes will shrink for the next two decades and may result in what's referred to as the *enrolment cliff* for the higher education sector.

The higher education sector, like many sectors of the economy, responds to changes in demand which itself is a function of demography. The US experienced the baby boom years after the Second World War. In 1957, 4.3 million children were born in the USA, a figure that will not be matched until 2050 even as the total population increases. This baby boom of almost 15 years, from 1945 to 1960, created a huge demand for higher education. Although the numbers in college-attending cohorts then declined, an enrolment fall-off was avoided because a higher proportion of high school graduates chose to go to college. In 1975, only 51 per cent went straight from high school to college;

by 1997 it was 67 per cent. From 1985 to 2007 the number of undergraduates across the country increased from 10.6 million to 15.6 million. Colleges expanded, constructed new buildings and hired more staff. By 2010 there were 18.1 million undergraduates at universities and colleges across the land. And then demography exerted its power. Because the number and proportion of students going to college had maxed out, college enrolment dropped and by 2019 it was down to 16.1 million. An eight-decade expansion is coming to an end. The most prestigious universities with a huge demand for a fixed number of places are unlikely to experience any decline. Declining enrolment is a much bigger issue for those higher-educational institutions further down the academic pecking order. The biggest impact is faced by those small private colleges that lack even a modicum of state support. Edinboro College in Pennsylvania had 8,642 students in 2011, ten years later it had 4,043. Small private colleges not considered to be in the top or even middle tier are particularly vulnerable. There may be a shift towards cheaper online education and more pronounced use of temporary staff. In other words, the landscape of higher education and the traditional college life of the last 70 years will be transformed by a changing demography.

SUMMARY

We now live in a world of low and declining birth rates. One major consequence is that population growth has slowed in many countries around the world, especially the more affluent countries. There are some positives to this declining growth rate. For example, in some cases it may strengthen the hand of workers in tight job markets. As the labour pool shrinks in size, employers may have to pay more for labour, especially skilled labour. On the other hand, lower population growth will tend to reduce economic growth. A lot of investment demand is driven by population growth, so low or stagnant population growth can lead to reductions in spending and what's been referred to secular stagnation. We will need to restructure our economic models to understand how we can maintain full employment and low inflation in the time of low population growth.

As population growth stalls and reverses, some governments craft policies to encourage childbearing through incentives. Others try to impose restrictions on abortion and contraception. Others try a combination of the two. At their least harmful, pronatalist policies can be a gentle nudge to shift behaviours with incentives. At their harshest, there are attempts to control women's bodies so that they have more children.

We can make two conclusions from the assessment of pronatalist policies across the globe. First, the most effective policies are those that make it easier and cheaper for woman to have children while also working. Improving childcare, for example, seems to work better than small financial incentives for women to have more children. More women are working to maintain effective household purchasing power, so it is important that government polices focus on making it easier for all women, and especially working women, to have and rear children. This can be done in a variety of ways, but investing in childcare, mandating parental leave and ensuring gender equality in the workplace, especially for mothers, are all policies that seem to have some effect.

Second, even the most successful incentives across the world have limited impact as birth rates continue to decline or remain low. Boosting birth rates seems beyond the ability of existing government policies. In higher-income countries, tax incentives have a limited effect, although they may have an influence in helping lower-income families with children. Public attitudes, social behaviours and the broader landscape of socioeconomic conditions all play a much larger role than government policies in shaping the birth rate. Neither coercion nor nudges seem to have a major effect in stopping the decline in birth rates. Higher birth rates reflect the ease with which societies allow women to combine careers with family obligations.

FURTHER READING

Declining birth rate
Bongaarts, J. 1998. "Demographic consequences of declining fertility". *Science* 282(5388): 419–20.
Demeny, P. 2015. "Sub-replacement fertility in national populations: can it be raised?" *Population Studies* 69: S77–85.
Doepke, M. *et al.* 2022. "The economics of fertility: a new era". NBER Working Paper No. 29948.

Jett, J. 2023. "China's population falls for first time in decades hampering its economic rise". NBC News. https://apple.news/ARNidTMJsR6u5I6xAiLbePg.

Kearney, M. & P. Levine 2022. "The causes and consequences of declining US fertility". Aspen Institute. https://www.economicstrategygroup.org/publication/kearney_levine/.

Nolin, D. & J. Ziker 2016. "Reproductive responses to economic uncertainty". *Human Nature* 27(4): 351–71.

Case studies

Froide, A. 2012. "Taxing bachelors and proposing marriage lotteries: how superpowers addressed declining birthrates in the past". *The Conversation*. https://theconversation.com/taxing-bachelors-and-proposing-marriage-lotteries-how-superpowers-addressed-declining-birthrates-in-the-past-164214.

Khazani, O. 2022. "Iran is urging people to have babies – and making life hard for those who don't want to". *Los Angeles Times*. https://www.latimes.com/world-nation/story/2022-09-14/iran-urging-people-have-kids-restricting-abortion-contraception.

McCurry, J. 2022. "Record number of young people in Japan rejecting marriage, survey shows". *The Guardian*. https://apple.news/AdQfDYsKEQlG7zluWLeKtfQ.

Nakachi, M. 2006. "N. S. Khrushchev and the 1944 Soviet Family Law: politics, reproduction, and language". *East European Politics and Societies* 20(1): 40–68.

Ransel, D. 2000. *Village Mothers: Three Generations of Change in Russia and Tartaria*. Bloomington: Indiana University Press.

Schaeffer, K. & C. Aragão 2023. "Key facts about moms in the U.S". Pew Research Center. https://policycommons.net/artifacts/3793127/key-facts-about-moms-in-the-us/4598953/.

Stevenson, A. & Z. Wang 2023. "China's population falls, heralding a demographic crisis". *New York Times*. https://www.nytimes.com/2023/01/16/business/china-birth-rate.html?smid=nytcore-ios-share&referringSource=articleShare.

Second demographic transition birth rates

Ramm, A. & V. Salinas 2019. "Beyond the second demographic transition". *Journal of Comparative Family Studies* 50: 75–97.

Tertilt, M. *et al.* 2022. "A new era in the economics of fertility". Centre for Economic Policy Research. https://cepr.org/voxeu/columns/new-era-economics-fertility.

Ripple effect

Carey, K. 2022. "The incredible shrinking future of college". *Vox*. https://www.vox.com/the-highlight/23428166/college-enrollment-population-education-crash.

7
The ageing population

GETTING OLDER

The world's population is getting older. In 1970, the global median age was 20. Fifty years later it had increased to 30. There are still "youthful" countries such as Niger with a median age of 14.5 years of age, a figure that has held constant over the last two decades. Compare that with Japan's 48.4. The ageing of the population is prevalent in countries with very low birth rates, low immigration rates and/or high emigration rates. Table 7.1 highlights the super-aged countries with a large percentage of the population aged over 65. They include

Table 7.1 Super-aged countries

Country	Percentage Aged over 65
Japan	29.9
Italy	24.1
Finland	23.3
Puerto Rico	22.9
Portugal	22.9
Greece	22.8
Germany	22.4
Bulgaria	22.4

Japan (29.9 per cent) and Italy (24.1 per cent). Japan's median age in 1950 was 20.2 and has effectively doubled. Italy's median age almost doubled from 27.5 in 1950 to 46.8 in 2020. Aged countries now include most of East Asia, Europe, North and South America and Australasia. While most rich countries are ageing, some are ageing faster than others, with East Asian and European countries ageing faster than the USA. By 2050, South Korea will have 39.6 per cent of people aged over 65 to overtake Japan's predicted 37.5 per cent. By 2050, almost 33 per cent of the population of Germany and Italy will be aged over 65, but only 21 per cent for the USA.

From 1950 to 2100, the world's population aged over 65 will rise from 5 per cent to over 16 per cent. Across the globe, population profiles are shifting from population pyramids to population pillars (see Figure 7.1). In the case of Japan, the profile has changed from a broad-based pyramid to an overhanging cliff. The country's population pyramid is shown in Figure 7.2.

Countries with the highest old-age dependency ratio – the number of people older than 64 relative to the number in the working population aged

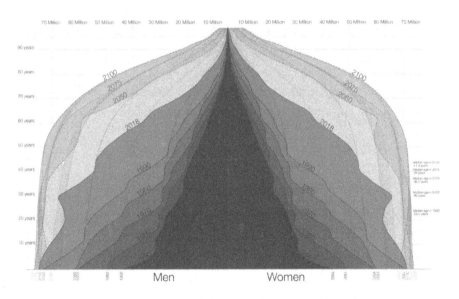

Figure 7.1 Global population profile

Source: United Nations Population Division – World Population Prospects 2017, https://ourworldindata.org/global-population-pyramid. Licensed under CC BY by the author Max Roser.

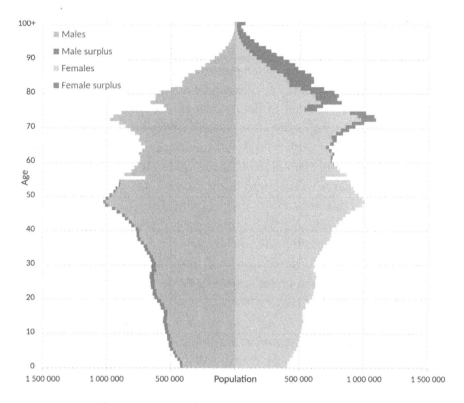

Figure 7.2 Population pyramid of Japan, 2021

Source: Statistics Bureau of Japan; Chart by Kaj Tallungs, https://commons.wikimedia.org/wiki/File:Japan_Population_Pyramid.svg. Licensed under the Creative Commons Attribution-Share Alike 4.0 International license.

14–64 – include Japan at 50.9 per cent, Italy at 37.1 and Finland at 37.1. Across much of Europe the figure rarely dips below 30 per cent whereas in 1950 it rarely peaked above 15 per cent.

The ageing of the population is caused by the fall in births and the increase in life expectancy. Variations in the rate and scale of ageing are a function of differences in birth rate, life expectancy and levels of population immigration and emigration. The "oldest" countries are those with the most marked fall in births and the longest lengthening of life expectancy. Japan is the world's "oldest" country because it has both a low birth rate of 1.3 and the world's longest life expectancy at 84.6 years at birth.

LIVING LONGER

People are living longer because of improved health outcomes owing to better health care and better nutrition. We can point to a whole host of specific improvements that have led to these circumstances, from improved food safety and safer working conditions to greater mechanization that shifts much of the heavy burden of work from people to machines. With mechanization and automation, fewer people are doing the physically demanding jobs that tend to shorten lifespans. Improved medical knowledge, which can identify diseases at a treatable stage, means that less people die at an earlier age from previously common killers such as cardiovascular diseases and cancer. Many diseases have been eradicated. More people experience a healthier childhood, which in turn leads to longer age spans. Current estimates suggest that life expectancy at birth in richer countries will reach close to 87 years by the middle of the twenty-first century.

People are not only living longer, they are leading more active lives. Lengthening healthy and active lifespans has transformed our understanding of what it means to grow old. To be sure, there are differences in life expectancy that reflect affluence and custom, but across the globe more people are leading healthier lives for longer. Most countries have seen an increase in life expectancy. The trend is most obvious in the richer countries, as shown in Figure 7.3. The two exceptions of Russia and the USA highlight some of the counterforces at work.

Russia and the USA

Life expectancy rate can sometime change in surprising ways. Russia's average life expectancy improved dramatically from 1945, when it was only 23.6 (a result of huge wartime losses), to 67.8 in 1965. Thereafter, there was a levelling off until the fall of the Soviet Union, when between 1992 and 1994 life expectancy at birth dropped by 6.1 years for men and 3.3 years for women. A major reason was the stress caused by the severe economic transition and the effects of excessive alcohol consumption, especially by men. By 2005, life expectancy had fallen to 64.9. There were deaths of despair during a period of economic dislocation and declining living standards. The gap between men's

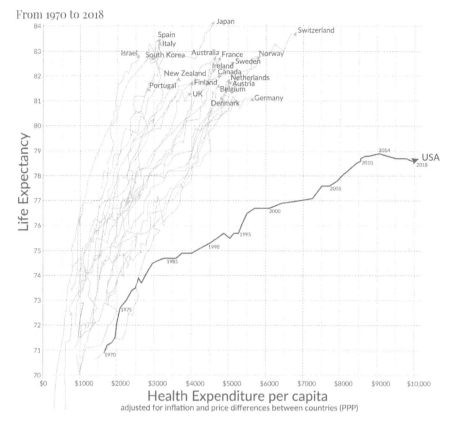

Figure 7.3 Life expectancy and healthcare spending

Source: Max Roser, Our World in Data, https://commons.wikimedia.org/wiki/File:Life_expectancy_vs_healthcare_spending.jpg. Licensed under the Creative Commons Attribution-Share Alike 4.0 International license.

and women's life expectancy widened dramatically. Thereafter, life expectancy began to improve, and by 2020 it had reached 72.9. It is sometimes referred to as the *Putin effect* since it is associated with the presidency of Vladimir Putin. It should more realistically be called the *resource effect* since Putin's presidency coincided with a rapid increase in the global price of oil and gas, which are Russia's main exports. This windfall filtered down to ordinary Russians. Continuing support for Putin, at least up until the invasion of Ukraine, is a function of the national sense of economic improvements embodied in the marked increase in life expectancy.

Figure 7.3 highlights how life expectancy in the USA was beginning to falter compared to other rich countries from around 1980. The slowing trajectory reached an inflection point in 2014 bending downwards. The actual decline in life expectancy in the USA began in 2015 and was driven at first by deaths from the opioid epidemic. The USA stands alone among its peers in terms of its relatively low level of life expectancy, which is lower than Turkey and Greece and well below that of Japan. Life expectancy in America over the past four decades has been lagging those of other rich nations. Italians, for example, can now live about five years longer than Americans. Despite being the most prodigious spender on health care, the USA ranks only above average in health outcomes with many countries poorer than the USA having a higher life expectancy. Why? What seems to be distinctive is not only the hundreds of thousands of deaths from the opioid epidemic but a new class divide that separates those with or without a college degree. Anne Case and Angus Deaton provide a detailed account of the increasing divide in their analysis of what they call "diseases of despair". Those without a college degree are more likely to be divorced, suffer from depression and drug abuse, have less access to medical and healthcare services and have more debilitating illnesses. Between 1990 and 2018, death rates for college-educated white non-Hispanics aged between 50 and 54 remained under 50 per 100,000. For the similar non-college-educated group, the figure rose to almost 200. The mortality rate for non-college-educated Americans increased fourfold. The greatest percentage increase was for white women without a college degree, especially for those living in small towns and rural areas. Many women had to bear the loads of holding families together at a time of rising unemployment and opioid addiction. Other societies experienced similar trends of deindustrialization, the decline of blue-collar jobs and widening inequality. However, most had stronger social safety nets with higher welfare benefits and better public health programmes that softened the downward spiral.

The higher mortality because of the Covid-19 epidemic meant that life expectancy dropped significantly, by 1.8 years from 2020 to 2021. The next year the fall was 0.9 years and the combined figures for the two-year period was the largest decrease since the 1920s. For Americans born in 2021, life expectancy declined to 76.1 years compared to an average of 79 years in 2019. The biggest drop was experienced by indigenous Americans, whose life expectancy in 2021 was 65.2 years, down a staggering 6.6 years from 2019. For Native

Americans, the decline was caused by higher Covid-19 death rates, overdose deaths and alcohol-related diseases such as chronic liver failure and cirrhosis. Covid-19 accounted for more than half the increase in deaths among whites in 2021, while unintentional injuries including overdoses accounted for about 12 per cent.

As Figure 7.3 shows, the USA spends more on health than any other country, which in 2021 reached nearly $13,000 per person, but has one of the poorest outcomes. A child born in the USA in 2019 is expected to live to 78.5. A Japanese child born in the same year is expected to live to 84.5 and in Sweden to 82.4. Money spent on health care in the USA is eaten up by burdensome administrative overheads, overpaid administrators and medical professionals, and costly procedures to satisfy insurance providers.

Other structural reasons behind the lower life expectancy in the USA, compared to its peers, include the lack of universal health care, greater prevalence of gun violence, lack of government support for childcare and an inadequate response to the Covid-19 pandemic. The flaws in the system were highlighted during the Covid-19 pandemic. Vaccine hesitancy in the USA was only partly responsible. A fractured public health system meant that Covid-19 killed more than a million Americans, and in 2021 it remained the third leading cause of death among Americans. The pandemic revealed a declining public health system that lags behind other countries that offer universal health coverage, more equitable access to medical services, greater investment in public health and much lower administrative costs. And while most countries in the world saw rising death rates because of the Covid-19 pandemic, most began to bounce back. One study found significant bounce-back from the losses of 2020 in countries in western Europe, while eastern Europe and the United States continue to have life expectancy deficits (Acholey *et al.* 2022)

National statistics can hide significant regional variations, and in the case of the United States this is significant. Life expectancy varies enormously across US regions, with the bicoastal metropolitan areas looking like Europe but the South and the Midwest doing much worse. The variations have been increasing. In 1990, Ohio and New York had similar life expectancy but now Ohioans live on average four years less than New Yorkers. In 2021, the estimated life expectancy for men in the USA was 77.2 but for Black men in Washington, DC, in contrast, it was 65.2 years, substantially lower than the average 73.6 years life expectancy for men in Bangladesh.

The reasons behind this variation include growing inequalities in wealth, which are translated into health statistics. The richer, more affluent groups tend to live in the big coastal metropolitan areas rather than the South and the Midwest. There are also policy differences. Some of the poorer states tend to be Republican-controlled and have refused to expand Medicaid. The richer, more affluent parts of the country tend to take a more proactive role in public health, which improves life expectancy, whereas the poorer parts tend to eschew public health interventions. The result is an increasing disparity in life expectancy.

AGEING COMPRESSION

The ageing of the population can be exacerbated by compression. Consider the case of Puerto Rico, where more than one in five residents are aged over 65. It has one of the highest shares of older adults in the world and is very similar to countries such as Japan, Italy and Germany. The ageing is a function of its very low birth rate of 0.9 births per woman but is also reinforced by emigration. There is ageing by compression because working adults leave the island to find better employment opportunities. Puerto Ricans can easily move to the USA. More than 700,000 residents have left in the past ten years. The high level of emigration is a function of diminishing economic opportunities at home. There are consequences to this selective outmigration. Puerto Rico exports its demographic dividend as the economically active leave the island, leaving behind a much older population. Many of those return to the island when they have retired, ageing the population even more. The elderly population has had a harder time coping with recent environmental disasters. In 2018, Hurricane Maria resulted in more than 3,000 deaths, the vast majority of whom were aged over 60. As the climate warms, and more frequent and larger hurricanes batter the island, an elderly population faces increased environmental vulnerabilities. There is a double whammy of an ageing population and increasing environmental risk. The US Congress has also imposed caps on Medicare and Medicaid in Puerto Rico, which are funded at lower rates. More than 30 per cent of the population live alone. Increasing severe storm activities are impacting seniors, many living alone in poor conditions and unable to cope as storms knock out power lines. Hurricane Maria and hurricane Fiona in 2022 exposed the vulnerability of the ageing population in Puerto Rico. The elderly are the most vulnerable population in a vulnerable region. Hector Cologne and Anna Serrano are in their eighties. Like many Puerto Ricans they moved to New York City to find work. They retired to the island but find it difficult to maintain their home in the wake of repeated storms. As Serrano told a reporter, "Puerto Rico is not made for the old" (Hernandez 2023).

Compression is also a major reason behind the rapid ageing of populations in eastern and southern Europe. Countries such as Greece, Hungary, Poland and Portugal also experience a selective outmigration of the younger, more economically active population who can easily move to the greater opportunities of other EU countries such as Germany and France. Even non-EU members in the region face similar demographic difficulties. Take the case of North Macedonia. It has a low birth rate of 1.3, but the ageing is also reinforced by the selective emigration of the younger, more economically active population. Over 30 per cent of the approximately 1.8 million Macedonians live in another country. There are over 100,000 in Germany, 66,000 in Switzerland and 63,000 in Italy. This migration was aided by the fact that Bulgaria, an EU member and close neighbour, allowed ethnic Macedonians to apply for Bulgarian passports that allowed them free entry to EU states. Unemployment in North Macedonia is high even by regional standards and wages have steadily declined. People have voted with their feet and the population fell from 2.02 million in 2002 to 1.86 million in 2021. Economic growth is hampered by this haemorrhaging of the economically active. A downward spiral of declining economic opportunities leads to outmigration that in turn leads to reduced economic activity, which stimulates ever more outmigration. North Macedonia, like many countries in southern and eastern Europe, has both an ageing and an emigrating population.

Ageing compression is a significant feature at the subnational regional level. Take the case of Japan. It is an aged and fast ageing country. However, the process has regional variations. As young people head for the cities, especially the big cities such as Tokyo, which now has a metro population of over 38 million, rural depopulation leads to an ageing and shrinking rural population. The number of farmers, for example, has declined from 12 million in 1960 to 2 million in 2015, with more than 70 per cent of them aged over 60. Many villages and small towns in rural Japan fall below the threshold for the efficient provision of basic services such as health, education and transport. At least 869 municipalities, almost half of the country's total, are at risk of vanishing altogether. Many are propped up by generous government subsidies. Some have responded by amalgamating nearby municipalities, while others embark on promotional plans to encourage tourism and immigration by promoting their quiet lifestyle and cheap housing. Ageing compression and population shrinkage in Japan, as elsewhere, has a distinct rural bias.

CONSEQUENCES

What are the consequences and responses to ageing? Let's consider four major elements.

Economic effects

An ageing population can dampen economic growth because there is a less economically active population. In 2021, 25 per cent of the population of Japan were aged 65 years and older. That is a dramatic increase from fewer than 5 per cent in 1950. China's working-age population, aged 16–55, numbered 882 million at the end of 2021, representing just over 62 per cent of the population down from 74 per cent in 2010. There are now 200 million people aged over 65 accounting for over 14 per cent of the population. In middle- and even some high-income countries, older people tend to have less income and so both consumption and investment can slump and per capita GDP can fall.

There are a variety of policy responses to the macroeconomic issues of ageing to avoid economic shrinkage. One way is to increase labour force participation, especially female participation rates. Governments can make it easier for women to both work and have children through making childcare affordable, ensuring gender equity in the workplace and making the workplace a more comfortable space for women and mothers. These policies can also increase birth rates because it allows women to have children without facing economic hardships. Sometimes the policies are implicit. Take the case of South Korea, where traditionally employees, and especially female employees, have been subjected to workplace harassment or bullying by superiors without much recourse. Women in particular face harassment, especially through mandatory office outings that involve dinner and alcohol. In 2019, two pieces of federal legislation were enacted so that workers in South Korea cannot be forced to drink alcohol at company outings or work more than 52 hours per week. This workplace anti-bullying legislation shifts the narrative about the culture of work and especially the role of women in the workplace.

Another way to offset a shrinking workforce is to improve the productivity of the available pool of labour. Improving labour productivity is a fundamental element of most government economic policies. However, the shrinking working population forces governments to think more carefully about how they can enhance and extend labour productivity so that a decline in the working-age population does not necessarily lead to a decline in overall productivity. Making people more productive is not simply about making them work longer hours but about making them more efficient through training and education, and making sure that a constant updating of skills is a lifelong opportunity. Another way is to increase the level of mechanization. The growing use of robotics in Japanese manufacturing plants is one response to growing labour shortages.

There are also harsher responses to promote labour force participation. Neoliberal responses tend to muscle labour force participation by reducing social benefits for the unemployed or requiring workforce participation from those receiving benefits. Republicans in the USA for example held up budget negotiations in 2023 with demands to enforce new and expanded work requirements for federal programmes for the poor. Able-bodied adults who do not live with dependents would be required to work or attend training programmes. Few studies show much positive economic impact of these proposals. They arise from heated political rhetoric rather than sober economic analysis. The politicians who advance these solutions are essentially signalling their conservative and anti-liberal credentials to their constituents and donor base.

Another way to deal with the shrinking workforce is to import labour. Australia, Canada and the USA have long relied on immigration to boost population and stimulate their economies. They have established rules and regulations to govern the import of labour. The ease of entry varies in response to economic conditions and populist backlash. The USA effectively cut off most immigration from 1930 to the mid-1960s. In general, immigrant societies find it easier to import labour because a strong immigrant narrative is part of the national identity. For some countries, the promotion of immigration to fill labour shortages is more recent. For West Germany, a labour shortage in the 1950s led to a guest worker programme that encouraged foreign workers, and today there are at least 7 million Turkish citizens living in Germany. Fellow EU members, especially from the former eastern Europe, then filled the German labour shortage. As Germany ages, 20 per cent of the population are aged over 65 and major labour shortages have returned, especially for skilled manufacturing workers. More recently, there has been a shortage of care professionals; for every 100 open job positions in elderly care there are generally only around 20 jobseekers. In 2019, the German parliament passed a law that provides incentives to attract non-EU workers.

South Korea has strict immigration policies but favours female marriage migrants who tend to have higher birth rates than native-born South Koreans. Marriage migrants account for a disproportionately higher share of live births. Foreigners now account for nearly 5 per cent of South Korea's population. A multicultural family support act passed in 2008 embraced the multiculturalism of female marriage migrants.

Filling a labour shortage is an economic issue, but encouraging immigration is a politically charged and culturally sensitive issue. For some countries there is strong resistance to encouraging immigration, especially from countries that are very different from their own. In countries with an ethnic homogeneity and little cultural diversity, immigration represents, for some, a possible threat to the cultural integrity of the nation. Japan has long resisted encouraging immigration. It has moved tentatively to encourage more immigration but the scale and rate of aging means than even encouraging migration to levels of political feasibility is unlikely to reduce Japan's old-age dependency ratio. In the short to medium term, Japan requires greater productivity and increasing labour force participation.

Encouraging immigration poses political challenges. Countries import "workers" but the people who arrive also have ethnicities and cultures, religions, values and customs that may not fully accord with the norms and practices of the host country. Encouraging immigration does not just fill a labour shortage, it also creates a new source of diversity and difference. On the one hand, this can be a source of dynamism and creativity. On the other hand, it can also provoke a backlash that can become pronounced when there are marked differences between immigrant groups and the host society or when economic growth stutters and falters. It is easy to then blame immigrants for a host of social ills. During economic recessions in particular, the idea of foreign immigrants taking scarce jobs becomes a powerful drive of populist, anti-immigrant rhetoric and politics. We can see this in the tenor of politics in European countries, from Austria and Switzerland to Hungary and the UK.

A variety of policies can be adopted to overcome labour shortages caused by increasing life expectancy and the aging of the population. As discussed above, workers can be imported as part of tailored immigration programmes. Generous paid leave policies could enable women to both have children and work in the labour force. The ageing of the population is not a guaranteed recipe for economic decline. A range of policies can be employed to increase the number of workers through increasing labour force participation, raising the retirement age, improving the productivity of the existing pool of workers through better training, education and lifelong learning and encouraging the immigration of workers. The demography of an aging population does not necessarily lead to the destiny of economic decline.

There are also some positive economic consequences of an ageing population. There is, for example, the development of a new "silver" or "longevity" economy. More elderly consumers now constitute a growing proportion of national and global markets. Meeting their needs is now a $9 trillion market in the USA. In the richer countries, growing old for many households does not necessarily mean getting poor. There is a significant affluent sector of the more elderly population. Some are concerned about purchasing experiences and the quest for self-actualization as well as the pursuit of consumer goods. The longevity economy is dominated by women since they outnumber men in the later stages of life – because they have a longer life expectancy – and tend to control household spending.

The longevity economy is not only fuelled by the high spending of affluent seniors but also includes the entrepreneurial talents of older people, many of whom can make a substantial economic contribution. This requires anti-ageist attitudes and sometimes legislation to fully exploit the resources in more elderly populations. While youthful vigour is often prized, ageing, while it may lead to a slowdown in the ability to process information, also brings the compensation of greater experience, a wider perspective and perhaps less hurried and error-prone decision-making.

Japan is at the furthest extreme of population ageing; a result of low birth rates, limited immigration and a long-life expectancy. Some commentators looking on the bright side use the term *silver demographic dividend* with reference to unlocking the untapped work capacity of an ageing population. Measures to promote this dividend in Japan include abolishing compulsory retirement and mandating employers to keep employees on the payroll until they reach the age of 70 if they wish to stay on.

An ageing population also has the capacity to unlock new sources of economic transactions. A second demographic dividend can occur because the ageing population often has enough savings and asset accumulation to invest and pass on to younger generations. This is especially true in countries, such as Norway and Sweden, with strong social welfare systems where the government picks up most of the tab for health care and income security for the retired. At its best, this second dividend can lead to a powerful source of consumption spending and investment. It can be undermined, however, when fiscal crises weaken income supports from the government and/or declining birth rates mean there are fewer children to look after ageing parents and grandparents. It is also threatened when there is a heavier reliance on private sector funding of retirement, little coverage of pharmaceuticals for the elderly and a higher proportion of private long-term care financing.

This second demographic dividend involves the intergenerational transfer of resources from the older to the younger generation. Consider the United States with 73 million baby-boomers (those born between 1946 and 1964); the youngest are turning 60 while the oldest are nearing 80. It is estimated that $84 trillion will be passed down between 2022 and 2045 from this cohort of older Americans to younger Americans (Smith 2023). The bulk of this wealth will be given and received by only around 10 per cent of the richest households. This wealth transfer will further increase inequality as those who receive substantial inheritances will be better positioned than those who do not. Social mobility works best when there is a level playing field. Inequality will grow with this massive intergenerational transfer of wealth as it will reinforce the division between the wealthy and the rest, making it difficult for younger generations of less affluent parents to do as well as those lucky enough to have rich parents and grandparents.

Paying for social welfare

Apart from the macroeconomic issues, there are problems in the financing of social welfare programmes as the population ages. In many societies social welfare programmes, such as old-age pensions or income support, are often provided by contributions from the wages of the working population. There is in effect a transfer of income from contributors to beneficiaries. When there is a change in ratio between the two groups there may be difficulties in funding the welfare programmes.

Take the case of the USA. Currently, 45 million Americans are aged 65 and by 2030 that number will reach 73 million, roughly one in five Americans. A baby born in 1900 had an average life expectancy of 47, one born in 1950 could expect to live to 68 and by 2019 this had risen to 79. An 80-year-old man in the USA can now expect to live to 88 and an 80-year-old woman until she is 90. The growing old-age dependency ratio is shown in Figure 7.4.

The three big social programmes – Social Security, Medicare and Medicaid – that benefit seniors rely on the contribution of the working-age population through payroll taxes. The ratio has changed as the population has aged. In 1960, the ratio was 5.1 workers to every beneficiary. By 2021 the ratio of workers to beneficiaries was 2.8 and is projected to decrease even further to 2.3 by 2035. Looking into the future there will be fewer workers to support each retiree as the population aged 65 and older is expected to increase to 24 per cent by 2060 while the proportion of the working-age population is expected to shrink from 62 per cent to 57 per cent by 2060. The problem may be exacerbated by Social Security's optimistic estimates of a rising fertility rate beginning in 2022 with a predicted TFR of 2.0 by 2040.

The funding issue can be solved by increasing the age of retirement, reducing benefits directly or indirectly through failing to keep pace with inflation or some combination of these. In the USA, the eligibility age of Social Security was raised from 65 to 67 in 1983 and there are proposals to raise the age to 70. There are no easy solutions since all of the proposals come with costs and political risks. One solution is to increase the age at which retirement benefits accrue. In practice, however, this has proved very problematic. In super-aged Italy for example, there are 34 retired pension recipients for every 100 workers, and by 2070 it will be 60 retirees for every 100 workers. A law established in 2011 proposed increasing the retirement age in stages to reach 67 in 2019. It

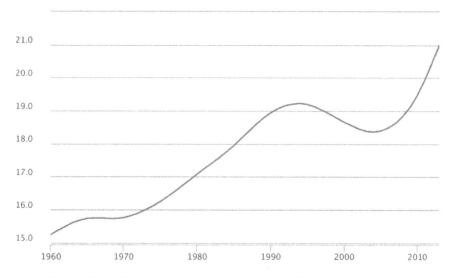

Figure 7.4 Old-age dependency ratio in USA (>64 to 15–64)

Source: World Bank, presented by BLUENOMICS, https://commons.wikimedia.org/wiki/File:US_old_age_dependency_ratio.png. Licensed under the Creative Commons Attribution-Share Alike 4.0 International license.

was extremely unpopular and was abandoned after a winning coalition fought the 2018 election on the promise to repeal it. Now a person is eligible for retirement benefits when their age plus their years of tax contributions to paying pensions equals 100. The funding of this programme, approximately US$7.5 billion, is one element behind Italy's ballooning debt. Government spending on pensions takes up over 60 per cent of Italy's GDP, more than any other Organisation for Economic Co-operation and Development (OECD) country apart from Greece. Unable to increase retirement age, Italy now has to look over the longer term to encourage women to have more children and over the shorter to medium term to relax immigration policy. Both are unlikely.

The governments of aged and ageing societies have sought to delay the age of formal retirement. This comes with a political cost. In France in 2022, the government's proposal to increase the age of eligibility for retirement benefits generated massive popular protest and street demonstrations. President Macron's government sought to increase the age of retirement from 62 to 64.

The figure is low compared to its European partners, but the age had become central to many people's notion of what the state owes its citizens. The low retirement age and high life expectancy mean that the French spend more time in retirement than most other countries, with the average French man typically spending 23.5 years in retirement compared to 20 years for men in Britain and Germany. Pension payments in France are also generous, with pension income roughly 58 per cent of pre-retirement levels compared to just over 50 per cent for Britain and Germany. One positive consequence is a very low level of poverty among retired people: only 4 per cent compared to the OECD average of 13 per cent. The government support is costly and Macron argued that raising the retirement age would cover a predicted €13.5 billion shortfall by 2030. The proposals motivated the French public enough to take to the streets in large numbers to protect their cherished retirement system, but the government was able to push through the unpopular policy and it became law in 2023, albeit at the cost of tremendous political capital. As another example, to deal with its ageing population China is planning to raise its retirement rate in phases. Currently it has one of the lowest retirement ages in the world: 60 for men, 55 for white-collar women and 50 for women who work in factories.

Raising the retirement age seems, on the face of it, a relatively simple fix. There are, however, two major problems. The first, as shown in the Italian and French examples, is the political resistance from a citizenry socialized into the idea of fixed retirement ages as a firm social contract between the governed and the governing. The second problem is the inequities involved in raising the age of retirement. Manual workers tend to have shorter lives than more affluent office workers, and they tend to work longer as they start work at an earlier age. Raising the age of retirement benefits thus has a more negative impact on lower-income and manual workers who often have hard and punishing jobs. They also tend to have less healthy post-retirement years so increasing the retirement age has a regressive impact that negatively impacts those who are poorer and on low incomes more than the affluent and wealthy. Consider the case of the USA where the rich tend to live 13 or 14 years longer than the poor. The health span – the length of time a person spends living without major illness or disability – is primarily a function of a person's socioeconomic status, so the rich get to retire and lead active lives while the poor may have more constrained lives. Increasing the retirement age to 70 for example is not such a burden for a sedentary office worker as it is for a person with a lifetime of work on a factory floor, in construction or in heavy manual labour.

In societies with an ageing population and weaker social security nets, the problems are magnified. China's problem is that it got old before it got rich. The growing elderly population in China raises concerns for the funding of even the meagre pension system. China's population aged over 60 is now 267 million, representing almost 19 per cent of the total population. Citizens over 60 years of age account for more than 20 per cent of residents in 13 of China's 30 provincial level jurisdictions. Ageing is now seen as a major challenge facing China in the coming years, and it will only worsen as birth rates fall and the population declines. With fewer workers contributing to the pension scheme of an increasing number of elderly people there is an opportunity for fiscal crisis. Shortfalls are likely to occur in the next two decades from even the modest levels provided now as the population aged over 60 is likely to exceed 500 million by 2050. There are enormous pressures on the elderly who live in urban areas. In rural areas the elderly rely more on their families for support.

Across the world, societies will have to cope with the problem of how to pay for the benefits given to an increasing elderly population from the wages of a declining working population. There are a range of solutions, from increasing the retirement age, reducing benefits or levying higher taxes. All of them, however, come with political costs and negative redistributional effects.

Political consequences

As they grow in size and wealth, through their own savings and welfare benefits, the older population can become an important political as well as economic factor. In many countries this is reinforced by two things. First, politicians, at least in democratic societies, respond to who votes. In general, older people tend to vote more than younger people and so politicians responding to electoral opinion tend to favour the needs of the elderly more than the young. Second, in many countries the form of electoral representation overvalues the elderly more than the young. Take the case of Japan where historically rural voters are overrepresented compared to those in the big cities. There are more electoral districts in the sparsely populated rural areas than the denser cities. Given the age profile of older rural areas and younger city populations, the elderly obtain a disproportionately large number of seats in parliament and hence greater political power. They benefit more from government largesse as politicians court the rural elderly vote with generous government spending and specific policies such as extensive subsidies to farmers. Rural voters tend to be older and more conservative, and this explains in part the continuing domination of the more conservative party who have been in power for much of the postwar era in Japan. Similarly in the United States, where each state has two senators irrespective of the size of the state. The smaller, more rural states with more elderly populations thus have an influence over and above their population size in national debates.

An "aged and ageing" agenda can emerge in the political arena as the population ages and organizes. The American Association of Retired People (AARP), with almost 38 million members, is a powerful interest group that focuses on the issues of those aged over 50. It is active in healthcare policy debates pushing for drug pricing reform, promoting AARP-branded health insurance and campaigning to strengthen Social Security and Medicare. It is an important player in national politics with a large membership, significant resources and effective outreach. The AARP also has wider goals when it promotes safe, walkable streets as well as age-friendly housing and transportation. These goals can often align with other age groups in the pursuit of less age-specific and wider goals such as healthier, fairer cities and making cities and neighbourhoods more liveable and walkable. Objectives can thus transcend the immediate interests of the aged. However, as debates about health care, retirement and welfare benefits occur in the context of a fiscal crisis, the promotion of the interests of the elderly may be at a cost to the younger population. In the USA for example, the federal budget will spend two-thirds of its budget over the next decade on the over-65 age group. We are more used to analysing conflict in terms of race, class and ethnicity, but in an ageing world we may be witnessing the beginnings of sharper divisions between age groups.

Although it is hazardous to summarize the attitude of entire generations, we can still make broad generalizations. Most surveys find that there is a variance of opinion between the elderly and the young. Older people are more likely to consider maintaining pensions and health care as the main political issues while the younger generations rate issues surrounding the environment, education and assisting the poor much higher. As a population ages and the older people play a larger role in setting the political agenda, we may be witnessing a shift away from redistributional policies. There is also the more general sense that as people get older, they often tend to look backwards. A politics of nostalgia is often the result. There is some evidence that the right-wing populist shift in many societies in western Europe and North America is in part driven by an ageing population who grew up in times of more affluence and greater ethnic homogeneity. They feel a sense of decline more acutely and tend to be more threatened by ethnic diversity than younger people. The right-wing nationalist shift in places such as the USA with the rise of Trump, Britain and the issue of Brexit or the authoritarian populism of Poland and Hungary are in part related to ageing populations whose political nostalgia is often expressed in authoritarian populism. There is a rise of anti-immigration populism in ageing societies (Dotti 2020).

Social consequences

All stages of the DT create a ripple of consequences. In the early stages it is the rapid population growth and increasing youth of the population that upends traditional patterns. In the latter stages it is the ageing of the population and the inversion of the population pyramid.

Much of the modern world was imagined and constructed around the idea and reality of a much younger population. Everything from the small print on tiny screens, designed it seems only for those with perfect eyesight, to traffic lights for pedestrians that assume people are walking at the speed of Olympic runners are examples of a world that pays little heed to an ageing population. And promotion of youth and vitality over age and experience continue to dominate our culture.

But as the world ages we need to adapt. We can perhaps look to the experience of the more aged countries that are adapting to this new normal. The adaptations can come in different forms, from opening malls earlier since old people like to walk early in the morning, discounts for seniors, infographics that are large and easy to read, provision of benches so that when people get tired they can take a break, elder centres in accessible public spaces, dementia assistance and prevention programmes, nursing robots, converting buildings to senior centres, making homes safer for seniors, age-friendly cities, age-friendly businesses and greater respect for elderly people. The list goes on and on. By 2050 the worldwide population of people aged over 60 is likely to be almost two billion out of nine billion.

A "senior shift" is inevitable. Sometimes it takes on a darker hue. As the population ages and there are more single-person households there is an increased possibility of what Koreans referred to as *"godoksa"* or lonely death, defined as when someone living alone dies and is only found after a certain amount of time. In 2021, in South Korea there were 3,378 lonely deaths, an increase from 2,412 in 2017. Men are five times more likely than women to experience a lonely death. There are now millions of ageing residents struggling to survive on their own and almost half of South Koreans aged over 65 are living below the poverty line. Thousands of elderly, isolated people are dying alone each year, their bodies undiscovered often for over a week. The problem has become so acute that a lonely death prevention and management act was passed by the central government that directed local governments to identify and assist residents at risk. The aged single person of limited means, in all societies, can easily fall through the social welfare net.

We are at the cusp of a new demographic of slowing growth and ageing populations. There is a lighter hue to the future if we can imagine the unlocked potential of an aged and ageing population.

SUMMARY

The world's population is getting older. The combined impact of declining birth rates and extending life expectancies is that we now live in a world inhabited by more older people. Asia is at the forefront of ageing. By 2050, the countries with the predicted highest share of people aged 65 and over are expected to include Hong Kong (40 per cent), South Korea (39 per cent), Japan (37 per cent) and Taiwan (35 per cent). There is also a slew of European countries also with marked ageing, including Italy (37 per cent), Spain (36 per cent), Greece (34 per cent) and Portugal (34 per cent). In all these countries the decline in birth rates is not made up by immigration and so the population will decline, which may negatively impact their economic performance. A country's ageing population also increases the growing disease burden, which in turn may slow economic growth and strain healthcare systems. Societies may be faced with a dramatic increase in the entitlement burden, as more of the elderly demand health care and social services.

On the other hand, an ageing population in the richer countries may create a second demographic dividend if their accumulated wealth can be used to stimulate economic growth. This second demographic dividend will involve an intergenerational transfer of resources, which is likely to lead to growing inequality since those with inherited wealth will have distinct advantages over those who do not.

The full impact of an increasingly elderly population on the economy, government financing, political attitudes and even the very nature of our built environment has yet to unfold. We are moving into a new demographic reality of slowing population growth, declining populations and ageing populations, with a set of experiences largely shaped in the context of population growth and a more youthful demographic profile.

FURTHER READING

Ageing
Agronin, M. 2018. *The End of Old Age.* New York: Hachette.
Applewhite, A. 2016. *This Chair Rocks: A Manifesto against Ageism.* New York: Celadon.
Coughlin, J. 2017. *The Longevity Economy: Unlocking the World's Fastest Growing, Most Misunderstood Market.* New York: PublicAffairs.
Super, N. 2020. "Three trends shaping the politics of aging in America". *Public Policy & Aging Report* 30(2): 39–45.

Life expectancy
Acholey, J. *et al.* 2022 "Life expectancy changes since COVID-19". *Nature Human Behaviour* 6: 1642–59.
Case, A. & A. Deaton 2020. *Deaths of Despair and the Future of Capitalism.* Princeton, NJ: Princeton University Press.
Couillard, B. *et al.* 2021. "Rising geographic disparities in US mortality". *Journal of Economic Perspectives* 35: 123–46.
Karabchuk, T., K. Kumo & E. Selezneva 2017. *Demography of Russia: From the Past to the Present.* London: Palgrave Macmillan.
Klobucista, C. 2002. "Life expectancy is in decline: why aren't other countries suffering the same problem?" Council of Foreign Relations. https://www.cfr.org/in-brief/us-life-expectancy-decline-why-arent-other-countries-suffering-same-problem.
Ney, J. 2023. "Life expectancy and inequality". American Inequality. https://americaninequality.substack.com/p/life-expectancy-and-inequality.

Consequences of ageing

Alesina, A. & F. Passarelli 2019. "Loss aversion in politics". *American Journal of Political Science* 63(4): 936–47.

He, L. & N. Li 2020. "The linkages between life expectancy and economic growth: some new evidence". *Empirical Economics* 58: 2381–402.

Maestas, N., K. Mullen & D. Powell 2023. "The effect of population aging on economic growth, the labor force, and productivity". *American Economic Journal: Macroeconomics* 15(2): 306–32.

Minkler, M. & C. Estes 2020. *Critical Perspectives on Aging: The Political and Moral Economy of Growing Old*. Abingdon: Routledge.

Second demographic dividend

Cai, F. 2020. "The second demographic dividend as a driver of China's growth". *China & World Economy* 28(5): 26–44.

Ogawa, N. *et al.* 2021. "Population aging and the three demographic dividends in Asia". *Asian Development Review* 38(1): 32–67.

Smith, T. 2023. "The greatest wealth transfer in history is here with familiar (rich) winners". *New York Times.* https://www.nytimes.com/2023/05/14/business/economy/wealth-generations.html.

8
Demographic narratives and moral panics

In this chapter I consider a selection of important demographic narratives that are often framed as moral panics. Demographic narratives are stories about demographic issues that inform public opinion and debates. A moral panic has been defined as a widespread feeling of fear that is commonly an exaggerated response to social issues. Moral panics often work their way through the media and moral entrepreneurs to influence public opinion. They take social concerns to the level of threat to the existing order. In this chapter I look at how some demographic narratives blend into moral panics. I examine four in particular: global "overpopulation", the "right" composition of national populations, the "threat" of specific cohorts and the idea of a decline of "family values".

OVERPOPULATION

In 1968 an entomologist at Stanford University, Paul Ehrlich, published a book called *The Population Bomb*. It became a bestseller; millions of copies were sold, and it became a very influential text for people trying to understand global demography. It was co-written with his wife Anne Ehrlich, but her name was dropped from the final text. The book was less a measured analysis and more a polemic with incendiary remarks such as "hundreds of millions of people are going to starve to death" and that "nothing can prevent a substantial increase in the world death rate". With this doomsday scenario of overpopulation leading to famine, pollution and social and ecological collapse, it moved up the bestseller list and had an influence on popular opinion that persists today. It heightened concerns about rapid population growth, especially in what was then called the Third World (what we would now call the global South).

Apart for the lack of social sensitivity and the inability to see human population dynamics as different from animal populations (a form of the biologizing of human behaviour common among other sociobiologists such as E. O. Wilson), it had a racial bias. The problem was configured as: there were too many people from the so-called Third World. The population problem, in this reading, was in effect too many Black and Brown people overwhelming not only their own societies but the earth's ability to cope. It had a deeply racist and neocolonial shading since the high environmental impact of the rich was not considered to be an issue, so the problem was seen as poor people of colour rather than affluent white folks exerting a heavier imprint on the ecosystem.

The book was written at a specific demographic moment when many countries in the global South were going through stages 2 and 3 of the DT with a rapid decline in infant mortality leading to high birth rates and rapid population growth. The book became part of an ensemble of studies and resultant programmes that were used by international organizations and national governments to legitimize policies used to force a decline in birth rates. By the 1970s and 1980s population control programmes were common across the global South. They ranged from community-based programmes to more coercive programmes of sterilization and mandated contraception. In India eight million men and women were sterilized in 1975 alone and many states in India required proof of sterilization before people could obtain water or ration cards or be given pay raises. China adopted the one-child policy that probably led to 100 million coerced abortions. Ehrlich did not advocate for brutal programmes but he did support sterilization.

Although written at a specific demographic moment, the book also harks back to the writings of Malthus and the idea that population would increase more than food supply leading eventually to scarcity and famine. It is an idea of long provenance and ultimately reflects a pessimistic view of an expanding population coming up against the fixed limits of food supply. While Malthus's was a class-based perspective concerned about the fecundity of the lower classes, Ehrlich's more recent neo-Malthusianism had an implicit and explicit racial bias. The fear, sometimes more implied than articulated, was that there were too many people of colour being born. The world was being swept away by a rising tide of the non-white, non-Caucasian "others".

There are two fundamental errors at the core of the Malthusian original and more recent neo-Malthusian arguments. First, it is not just sheer population numbers that have an environmental impact but the size of the ecological footprint. Paul and Anne Ehrlich, standing in for affluent people in the West living in a detached house driving two cars, their home air conditioned in summer and heated in winter, created a larger ecological footprint than slum dwellers in Mumbai living in self-made housing with few amenities or facilities. The real environmental problem was not that there were too many people but there were too many rich people imposing a heavy cost on the carrying capacity of the earth.

Second, the basic idea of overpopulation in relation to a fixed food supply were just plain wrong. Esther Boserup, a Danish economist, took a different perspective. She argued that population growth, rather than coming up against fixed limits, spurs innovation and technological improvement. Rather than agriculture productivity determining population, it is population that determines agricultural productivity. Population growth and high population densities spur agricultural innovations such as irrigation and fertilizer use. Agricultural productivity intensifies as population pressure mounts. Her arguments are more in line with what has happened. There have been increases in the food supply because of increasing agricultural productivity as the population has expanded.

This is not to say that famine has been averted. Food shortages do occur around the world, but generally famines occur not because of the lack of food but the poor and inadequate distribution of food supplies. The work of Amartya Sen, for example, highlights that lack of food is not the cause of famine, it is social dislocation and political collapse. There are still people in the world facing food insecurity and too many people go to bed hungry at night, but invariably this is a social issue about the distribution of existing resources. It is not the basic supply of food that is the problem but the allocation of existing food resources in varying amounts to different groups of people.

The American economist Julian Simon provides an alternative to a dismal Malthusianism. He argued in a series of articles and books against a Malthusian catastrophe. More people were not the problem but, in his view, the solution. Rather than concentrating on resources and resource scarcity he tended to focus on the innovation and invention of people. The more people there are the more innovation occurs and the greater our ability to switch resources and improve productivity. The ultimate resource, according to Simon in a book with that title, is the human population.

There is now a vigorous debate between those who counsel control of the population and those who have a much more cornucopian view of a world of infinite resources. In reality of course it is much more complex than such simple arguments allow; so, let me summarize this section with three specific points.

First, some of the overpopulation arguments are charged with class and racial attitudes that tend to see other people as a problem. We should be aware of this bias. The panic concerns not so much the size of the population but the nature of the people having children. The strictures always seem to apply to them not us; you not me. The issue of the appropriate rate of global population growth becomes a panic when it is wrapped around class and racial prejudices.

Second, Boserup's argument, rather than that of Malthus, has been vindicated. Population growth has stimulated agricultural productivity rather than come up against the limits of a fixed food supply. The very real issues of food supply, food insecurity and hunger are more accurately described and addressed from social and economic perspectives. When we simply ascribe demography as the issue, we neatly sidestep more fundamental criticisms of the existing socioeconomic system.

Third, there are very real issues about the role of population in a sustainable world. Figure 8.1 shows the different future projections for global population. It is likely to plateau by 2080 at around ten billion, although notice how a difference of plus or minus 0.5 births per women will change the total from 14.5 billion to 6.2 billion by the end of this century. Whatever the future level, the more people there are with larger ecological footprints, the more the world is impacted. Pollution, resource depletion, climate change, decline in biodiversity and the possibility of massive species extinction are all very real problems heightened by increasing population and affluence. But they are not problems simply of the level of population but about how this population interacts with the world. Affluent consumers in the West, with their massive carbon footprints and guzzling of resources, are arguably more of a problem than the

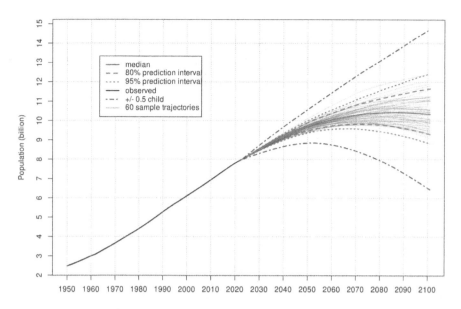

Figure 8.1 Global population projections

Source: 2022 United Nations, DESA, Population Division, https://commons.wikimedia.org/wiki/File:World_Population_Prospects.svg. Licensed under Creative Commons license CC BY 3.0 IGO.

growing populations of the global South. There is a population problem, but it's not simply about the size of the population, it's more about how this population lives in the world. The human environmental footprint is a function of population, affluence and technology. To create long-term sustainability, we need to refashion the population–environment relationship. The size of the global population is a factor but not the only one. As we look towards the end of this century, the global population will fall from its current levels, but the way people interact with the environment still needs to be restructured to avoid the destruction of our planet's survivability.

THE "NATIONAL" POPULATION

The French writer Renaud Camus published a book in 2012 entitled *La Grand Remplacement* (*The Great Replacement*), in which he argued that in Europe, and especially France, non-white immigrants, with higher birth rates, were replacing traditional, white Europeans.

The idea of a great replacement of white people by what were described as non-white people is over a century old. Charles Pearson's 1892 book, *National Life and Character*, presented a picture of white people being "elbowed and hustled and perhaps even thrust aside". A New York lawyer, Madison Grant, published *The Passing of the Great Race* in 1916. It presented an apocalyptic vision of the decline and extinction of America's "Nordic" stock by non-Protestant immigrants. He was not a voice in the wilderness but an influential commentator whose ideas influenced eugenic policies, including forced sterilization laws in 31 states, and a change to the more restrictive federal immigration policies of the interwar period. His ideas travelled far across Europe, and he had a direct influenced on the Nazi regime's racial ideas and racist policies. The ideas continue to resonate. Tucker Carlson was a very influential and important commentator on Fox News in the USA, at least until his abrupt firing in 2023, who regularly espoused ideas of the replacement. He promoted the argument that foreign immigration was encouraged by Democratic politicians to maintain a voting bloc to keep them in power.

In many countries, especially those with relatively high levels of immigration, the character of the national population is changing. Consider the case of the USA. The dominant power bloc of the nineteenth century was white, male, Protestant Christians. In the era of mass immigration from roughly 1880 to 1920, the population became more varied, with more Catholics, Jews and Asians. The change provoked anxiety among the elite and the production of such works such as *The Passing of the Great Race*. A second wave of mass immigration began in 1970, again changed the character of the national population and again prompted racial anxiety. The white share of the US population has been dropping from a huge majority of 90 per cent in 1950 to 60 per cent in 2020 and will probably dip below 50 per cent by 2050. The trend has provoked fears by white nationalists and others that the country is changing for the worse. Behind this trend are differences in birth rates for white women compared to Latina women. And whites are not increasing their proportion because much of the immigration into the country is from non-whites. So we have an ageing white population and a more youthful minority population. The USA will never be a white population again. One reaction to this trend is the emergence of a more racist xenophobia.

Ideas have consequences. In October 2018 a man committed mass murder at a Pittsburgh synagogue. In May 2022, a man shot ten people – all African Americans – at a supermarket in Buffalo in New York State. Both were firm believers in the great replacement conspiracy theory and saw Blacks and Jews as threats to white Christian dominance. These are the extreme cases, but there are other examples of this demographic panic, whether it is in the way that the UK's Brexit issue was framed or in the wider adoption of ethno-nationalism and populist authoritarianism in countries around the world. A recurring idea is of a "pure" national population under threat from the "other" and too much foreign immigration as tantamount to national identicide. It contains imagery of a "pure" national stock being contaminated and ultimately replaced by another group with different beliefs and values. It is expressed in nativist sentiments, incendiary rhetoric, anti-immigration feelings and immigration policies that seek to limit entry. This cultural argument sometimes comes up against economic realities, especially in ageing societies. Even more closed-off societies, such as Japan, have come to realize that their economic future may perhaps lie in encouraging more foreign immigration. The declining birth rate in ageing populations of much of Europe may necessitate more foreign immigration but will come up against rising anti-immigration sentiment. While economic studies may show how immigration can be good for a country in terms of increasing the workforce, providing a younger labour force and perhaps generating a larger pool of entrepreneurial talent, they often only have limited purchase against cultural anxiety, which is keenly felt in ageing, low-growth societies. The great replacement theory is just the more extreme version of this cultural anxiety.

We are moving into a world where, on the one hand, we have ageing societies with shrinking labour pools and, on the other, countries with an oversupply of young labour compared to existing employment opportunities. This is the basic dynamic and driving force behind much of international migration. But immigration is not simply an economic transaction of workers filling vacancies; it has major social and cultural effects, especially when there are cultural differences between sending and receiving countries. There are genuine concerns and difficult conversations about issues such as assimilation, multiculturalism and the future make-up and character of national populations.

TROUBLESOME COHORTS: YOUTH BULGES AND SILVER TSUNAMIS

Although they do not have the same resonance and passion as the so-called overpopulation debate or debates about immigration, narratives about certain cohorts at times can take on the feel of a moral panic. Here we look at two of these. The first is the idea of a youth bulge as a major cause of social conflict. Many popular commentaries about the Arab Spring locked on to the idea of the youth bulge as a major cause of the social uprising. To be sure, many young, unemployed people who are overeducated for few job opportunities is not a recipe for social peace. However, some of the discussions about the youth bulge have too mechanistic a view that it is simply the large number of young people that is the incendiary issue. It is reminiscent of the context for the first study to employ the term moral panic, Stanley Cohen's 1972 analysis of youth culture in Britain in the 1950s and 1960s. It was a time of a youth bulge and more young people with more disposable income. A more conservative, middle-aged population looked askance as young working-class men were able to purchase a range of consumer goods including motorcycles and scooters. The class anxiety of the older, conservative population saw these young people as a threat to the social order. When youth cohorts become significantly large there is always some concern voiced by the older generation worried at this generational shift. "Youth as a problem" has for centuries been a staple of social commentary. It takes on greater urgency when the youth cohorts are particularly large, hence exerting more influence by sheer weight of numbers and especially at times of economic uncertainty and social dislocation. It is true that a large amount of young people in sclerotic economies is a cause for some concern. But it's not the youth bulge itself that is the issue, it is the way that the economy is structured and the society is organized.

At the other end of the age spectrum there is this sometimes alarmist debate about the growing size of the more elderly population. There are very real concerns about the economic implications of ageing societies and especially about paying for a growing number of people from the wages of a shrinking number of workers. However, the debate can often degenerate into a form of ageism. There are too many old people, assumes one narrative, and that will lead to fiscal crisis and economic decline. The narrative is tightly bound to traditional notions of productive and unproductive ages, the young and vigorous compared to the elderly and decrepit. We need to free ourselves from this mechanistic notion that links economic productivity only to certain cohorts. As we move into a new normal of a more elderly world, we need to keep an open mind on how we consider the relationship between economic productivity and age. This is not to skirt pressing issues about the economic costs of ageing societies, or about the need to age proof our cities and neighbourhoods.

We do need a debate about the consequences of ageing societies. And we require policies that encourage successful ageing through the avoidance of disease and disability, the maintenance of high cognitive and physical functioning and an engagement with life. The importance of encouraging volunteering, for example, is likely to keep people busy and engaged. Connecting with others and encouraging human interaction is likely to be one of the most significant public health responses to an aging population. People need to preserve purpose. There are also public health measures and much more vigorous public education campaigns about not smoking, regular exercise, healthy diet and moderate alcohol and drug consumption.

Even the much-hyped narrative about how to pay for the welfare state in ageing societies needs to be unpacked from its more sensationalist accounts. Social Security in the USA is the main form of government support for the elderly. A closer inspection of the mechanism reveals social choices that can avoid apocalyptic collapse. The funding for Social Security comes from payroll tax. However, that payroll tax is capped. In 2022, for example, the cap was set at annual earnings of $147,000. The system does have a shortfall but that is the result of rising inequality. A growing share of overall income has gone to people with really high incomes whose earnings above the cap are not subject to payroll tax. It also means that lower-income groups pay tax on a much higher proportion of their earnings than the rich and very rich. Social Security can be funded through a combination of moderate tax hikes and increases in the earnings cap. The moral panic about ageing turns out to be less an unavoidable demographic crisis than an opportunity to rethink income redistribution and taxation policies.

The more fevered arguments about a silver tsunami simply washing away economic growth potential are, I think, overblown. Worries about the increasing number of old people can at times take on the form of a demographic panic. We are moving into a new normal of ageing societies. Whether it is a graceful ageing recognizing the talents and contributions of the older generations or a more awkward ageing filled with problems and tensions depends on our collective actions and finding equitable and lasting responses to how we deal with generational differences. Demography is not destiny.

FAMILY VALUES

There are a range of demographic panics that centre around what can be termed "family values".

The birth rate is plummeting around the world below the replacement rate of 2.1 births per woman. This is a demographic tendency that is turned into a demographic panic when it is associated with a decline in the traditional family unit of a married couple with children. The patriarchy was built on a foundation of women having children and lots of them. The very large and rapid decline in birth rates upends this traditional role of women as wives and mothers. Debates about the birth rate can at times turn into a moral panic about "family values" and the role of women.

In China, single women are not allowed to freeze their eggs or undergo in vitro fertilization, and are routinely denied the care and services available to married women. This is in a country that has a pressing concern with falling birth rates. China is not unique. Many countries still have financial incentives, laws and legal structures that promote the combination of marriage and children. Despite the political reification of the family as fundamental unit, there is a trend towards more single mothers and fewer women having children.

Increasing numbers of young people say they don't intend to get married. A government-funded research institution in Tokyo, the National Institute of Population and Social Security, announced that the results of a 2021 survey showed that over 17 per cent of men and 14 per cent of women aged 18–34 said they had no intention of ever getting married. This were the highest figures since the questionnaire was first conducted in 1982, when only 4 per cent of women said they would never marry (McCurry 2022). The number of marriages continues to fall to just over half a million, the lowest figure since the end of the Second World War, as more young women want to remain single and have a career. Similarly in South Korea, where more young people are deciding not to get married, the term *"bihon"* has gained popularity (roughly translated as "willingly unmarried"). More people are ignoring the "big 30" deadline as it was called as a time to get married and start a family. Now 40 per cent of households in South Korea consist of just one person. Marriage rates and fertility rates and now at the lowest they've ever been.

For many traditionalists, the decline in the marriage rate is a cause for concern. However, it is not a function of "moral decline" as much as the moral entrepreneurs would have us believe. More women are deciding against marriage, especially early marriage, because they cannot easily combine a career with having children. Many households require multiple breadwinners and yet women suffer unequal pay, harassment and fewer promotional opportunities. And since many women are primarily responsible for most domestic labour they often shoulder a double burden. Remaining single or having fewer children avoids many of the problems. For young men, remaining single takes some pressure off being the breadwinner for an entire family. Discrimination against the unmarried, and especially unmarried women, is especially acute when marriage is a guiding framework for citizens to gain social benefits. Many governments allocate more generous benefits to traditional family units.

A decline in the marriage rates does not necessarily lead to a decline in birth rates. Another trend is the increase in the number of children born to single mothers and non-married couples. Around the world almost 56 per cent of children are now born out of wedlock. There is tremendous variation. Most children are born to married couples in Japan. Less than 1 per cent of births occur outside of marriage in China compared to almost 70 per cent of births in Iceland. Countries with more than half of children born outside of marriage include Mexico, France, Denmark, Sweden, Norway and Chile. Even in the ostensibly more religious USA, almost 40 per cent of births occur outside of marriage, an increase from 28 per cent in 1990. In some countries, children born to single-person households are more likely to be poorer than their married counterparts. But in regions such as Scandinavia, which have better childcare as well as a greater acceptance of unmarried partners as parents, there is no clear relationship between poverty and single parenthood. In most Scandinavian countries, a majority of children are born to unmarried partners. In many middle-income countries, a large portion are born to single mothers. Even as illegitimacy loses its stigma it is still often associated with legal discrimination in many countries. Yet it is becoming more common and accepted. Over 40 per cent of births in Europe are outside of marriage, but there are still countries such as South Korea where only 2 per cent of birth are to unmarried mothers. Since married women have more limited employment opportunities and little likelihood of having a child outside of marriage, more Korean women are neither getting married or having children.

Illegitimacy is a demographic panic that is disappearing. While long considered a sign of sinful, wanton behaviour, with corresponding restrictions and punishments for unmarried mothers, it is becoming more common and accepted. Over 60 per cent of births in France now occur outside of marriage; children born to married couples are the minority. Even in Ireland, long dominated by a conservative Catholic Church, out of wedlock births now constitute almost 38 per cent of all births. The USA and UK have illegitimacy rates of 37 per cent and 33 per cent respectively, with the USA having a higher rate of children born to single mothers, at 29 per cent compared to the UK's 23 per cent.

Changing family formations are so widespread that some have argued that, in some parts of the world, we are moving to a second DT. A transition marked by below replacement fertility, fewer marriages and more divorces, non-child couples, single mothers and unmarried couples with and without children. The traditional and often idealized family unit of a married couple with children is fast becoming a minority. The faster this change occurs the greater the backlash expressed in narratives and sometimes panics about a decline in "family values".

Illegitimate births were once a pervasive demographic panic, eliciting moral outrage and the shaming of single mothers. Once it was associated with "fallen women", with opprobrium being especially harsh for lower-class women. Today in many countries it has lost its power to evoke general outrage. It is no longer associated with condemnation apart from the lingering narrative of teenage mothers.

In the USA, from around 1960 public concern was expressed about the teenage mother. It was both a moralistic concern about children being born out of wedlock to young women and also an economic concern that the resultant offspring were more dependent on welfare. Teenage mothers were seen as deviant citizens. It also had a distinct racial bias as most of the teenage mothers represented in the media were young Black women. Teen pregnancy was encased in ideologies about ideal family forms, race and reproduction. What is interesting, however, is how the debate and the issue has in large part

DEMOGRAPHIC NARRATIVES AND MORAL PANICS

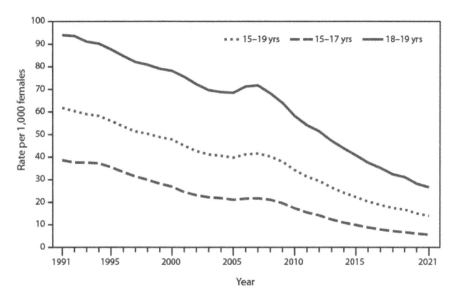

Figure 8.2 Teen births in the USA, 1991–2021

Source: National Center for Health Statistics, National Vital Statistics System, Natality Data, 2021, https://blogs.cdc.gov/nchs/2023/01/20/7245/ and https://www.cdc.gov/mmwr/volumes/72/wr/mm7203a8.htm.

disappeared. The teen birth rate, expressed as the number of mothers per 10,000 women aged 15–19, declined from approximately 90 in 1960 to 13.9 by 2021. Figure 8.2 shows a similar decline for different age categories in this cohort. The sharp decline was the result of more effective use of contraceptives, more information about pregnancy prevention, a reported decline in the sexual activity of teenagers, more federal funding for family planning and a growing discussion of the problems associated with teen pregnancies in the mass media. There was also a reinforcing downward spiral because teenage mothers tend to be daughters of teenage mother, so a decline in teenage mothers has a rippling effect. There's still a concern in the United States that there is a linkage between teenage mothers and poverty and the associated consequences for the children. The issue has not completely disappeared, but it has lost its potency in national conversations. The idea of the teenage mother as victim is sometimes replaced by issues of young female agency. And as teenage pregnancy becomes less connected to simple projections of race and class, it loses its potency as a moral panic. However, there remains the nagging problems of low-income single mothers in a less than supportive social welfare system and the negative lifelong impacts on their children.

The weakening of the moral panics of illegitimacy and teenage mothers highlights the shifting nature and changing dynamics of demographic panics. As society changes and attitudes shift, what was once seen as a problem, eliciting a moral panic, disappears or becomes an everyday reality that is taken for granted. It reminds us that demographic panics are less about demographics and more about social issues and political attitudes. Demography does not create panics, it provides the justification for them.

SUMMARY

Demographic discussions can often move out from narrow academic debates into wider popular discourse. When they become part of charged political debates, they can take on the form of a moral panic, which is a widespread feeling of irrational fear often focusing on the "other" as a source of demographic concern. In this chapter we looked at several moral panics. The first was the issue of overpopulation, especially as applied to the rapid population growth of the global South. Many of these debates drew upon the basic ideas propounded by Malthus about the relationship between population growth and food supply. Simply put, Malthus was wrong. His ideas are like a demographic zombie that refuses to die. While there were real concerns about very rapid growth hindering economic development, there was also racist and classist overtones that saw the problem as too many people of colour. Much of the overpopulation debate was encased in this racist container of understanding. There are issues regarding the population–resources relationship, especially as more of the world becomes affluent, as the heaviest footprint per capita is to be found among the richest countries of the world. A vital discussion is needed about the most sustainable population level and its environmental impacts, but this is more complex and more subtle than easy slogans such as "the population bomb" that draw upon incorrect Malthusian assumptions.

The second demographic moral panic centres on the issue of the change in character of national populations. In many countries around the world the religious, ethnic, racial and cultural mix is becoming more heterogeneous as a result of immigration. For some this poses an almost existential crisis about core national identity. And again, there may be legitimate concerns about the assimilation of diverse people into a shared culture. However, there is also an ugly, xenophobic rhetoric that centres on immigrants as a source of national decay.

In more recent years, demographic moral panics have also merged regarding different bulges in the population pyramid. Many see the youth bulge, for example, as a source of social unrest and political conflict. For others, the rapid increase in the elderly population is a probable cause of economic decline and fiscal overspending. However, as I have shown, the bulges do not mechanistically produce problems, and if carefully handled they can provide opportunities. So, it is not the bulges themselves but how we deal with them that will shape the future.

Finally, we considered narratives about the decline of family values that include fears of declining birth rates, the decline in marriage rates and growing illegitimacy. These are panics that emanate from specific ideas about morality. What is most noticeable, however, is that they are less related to a decline in moral values and more the collective result of individual decisions based on current realities. In many ways these new demographic trends reflect the direction of dominant cultural values rather than the majority values of the past. When freed from religious and governmental controls, people choose a variety of family forms.

FURTHER READING

Moral panics
Cohen, S. 1972. *Folk Devils and Moral Panics*. London: MacGibbon & Kee.

Overpopulation
Boserup. E. 1981. *Population and Technological Change: A Study of Long-Term Trends*. Chicago: University of Chicago Press.
Ehrlich, P. 1968. *The Population Bomb*. New York: Ballantine.
Simon, J. 1981. *The Ultimate Resource*. Princeton, NJ: Princeton University Press.
Simon, J. 2019. *The Economics of Population Growth*. Princeton, NJ: Princeton University Press.
Sen, A. 1980. "Famines". *World Development* 8(9): 613–21.

National populations

Ekman, M. 2022. "The great replacement: strategic mainstreaming of far-right conspiracy claims". *Convergence* 28: 1127–43.

Ramirez, S. 2023. "Great replacement or slow white suicide?" *Philosophy Today* 67: 171–88.

Toft, M. 2010. *The Geography of Ethnic Violence: Identity Interest and the Indivisibility of Territory*. Princeton, NJ: Princeton University Press.

Ageing

Goodhart, C. & M. Pradhan 2020. *The Great Demographic Reversal: Ageing Societies, Waning Inequality, and an Inflation Revival*. London: Palgrave Macmillan.

Harper, S. 2014. *Ageing Societies*. Abingdon: Routledge.

Youth bulge

Pruitt, L. 2020. "Rethinking youth bulge theory in policy and scholarship: incorporating critical gender analysis". *International Affairs* 96: 711–28.

Sydiq, T. & M. Tekath 2022. "Youth as generational configurations: conceptualizing conflicts along generation-based dynamics". *Peacebuilding* 10: 51–65.

Family values

Bute, J. & L. Russell 2012. "Public discourses about teenage pregnancy disruption restoration and ideology". *Health Communication* 27: 712–22.

Chiappori, P. 2020. "The theory and empirics of the marriage market". *Annual Review of Economics* 12: 547–78.

Hartley, S. 2022. *Illegitimacy*. Berkeley: University of California Press.

Kelly, D. 1996. "Stigma stories: four discourses about teen mothers, welfare, and poverty". *Youth and Society* 27: 421–49.

Livingston, E. & D. Thomas 2019. "Why is the teen birth rate falling?" Pew Research Center. https://www.pewresearch.org/short-reads/2019/08/02/why-is-the-teen-birth-rate-falling/.

Torche, F. & A. Abufhele 2021. "The normativity of marriage and the marriage premium for children's outcomes". *American Journal of Sociology* 126(4): 931–68.

Sassler, S. & D. Lichter 2021. "Cohabitation and marriage: complexity and diversity in union-formation patterns". *Journal of Marriage and Family* 82(1): 35–61.

9

Demography and contemporary challenges

Demography plays an important although often hidden role in contemporary global change. In this chapter I examine some of the ways in which demography is entangled in certain significant shifts in the global order: climate, political economy and geopolitics.

DEMOGRAPHY AND CLIMATE CHANGE

Because of the importance of human activity in shaping earth systems, some commentators have described a new geological age, the Anthropocene. Increasing population with growing per capita environmental impact has transformed the world. We have cleared the forests, reduced habitats and diminished biological diversity. And because of our use of fossil fuels, we have modified the climate. Our planet is warming to such an extent that we can identify a new subcategory of the Anthropocene: the Pyrocene.

Demography plays an important role in this new era. In one sense it has created the new era. The steady increase in global population in association with a large and an increasing per capita carbon footprint has generated enough greenhouse gases to change the climate regime to one that is warmer and more vulnerable to extreme climate events. The 100-year flood turns into a five-year flood, punishingly hot summers become commonplace and the once in a generation hurricane becomes a more regular event.

The current demographic distribution of population was based on a different climate regime. A world in which major floods were irregular events and extreme warming in many regions was rare. The current population distribution is now faced with a different set of conditions. These include but are not limited to the very rapid warming in cold latitudes, extreme warming in the mid-latitudes and a greater risk of sea level rise and flooding in river basins and coastal regions around the world. The current global population distribution was better suited to past climate regimes and is now faced with greater vulnerability because of the greater frequency of extreme weather events. It has resulted in various forms of climate refugee population movements. In Bangladesh, for example, residents are being flooded out from many of the rural areas by more powerful monsoonal rains and greater glacial melting from the Himalayas washing away their farmland. People are forced out, thereby exacerbating population pressures in the big cities, especially Dhaka. For many people around the world environmental conditions have worsened, as the land dries and the crops die in rural areas, the urban heat island effect means the big cities are getting hotter and the risk of flooding increases. Most of the burdens are disproportionately imposed on the more vulnerable.

Health is impacted in the Anthropocene. Life expectancy across the globe is decreased by 2.3 years because of exposure to pollution. There is substantial variation, with a 0.6-year reduction for those in the USA compared to 6.8 years for those in Bangladesh. Heat-related deaths are increasing to alarming levels. In Europe almost 62,000 people died in the summer of 2023 from heat-related deaths. In Phoenix, 300 people died in a 2023 heat spell that reached 43°C (110°F) for 31 consecutive days. The Pakistani cities of Jacobabad and Hyderabad now have 129 and 80 heat days respectively where temperatures are 32°C in the shade. Things will only get worse in the coming years. Belem in Brazil is estimated to have 222 days with extreme heat by 2025.

We have transformed our environment to such an extent that we have reduced the zones of habitability and made an increasing number of people more vulnerable to extreme weather events. The greatest burden is often faced by the poorest, who had the smallest role in global warming. Take the case of the numerous Pacific Island nations, which have some of the lowest carbon footprints in the world; they are now faced with the existential crisis of sea level rise that will inundate their territory.

Consider the case of Egypt, where family planning is now directly linked to combating climate change. The government has pursued a policy of encouraging families to have no more than two children. High birth rates are now seen as a national security issue. The fertility rate is declining but not fast enough. Egypt's population nearly quadrupled from 1960 to 2020. Large families are common in the rural areas where children are seen as a source of labour. The government has framed the debate in terms of a national security issue in relation to climate change, as rising temperatures increase the threat to the country's food and water supplies. Egypt is vulnerable to sea level rise, water shortages and extreme weather including heat waves and dust storms. The large and growing population is creating water scarcity, depleting natural resources and straining social services. Climate change is putting extra pressure on the Egyptian government, and indeed on governments all around the world, especially in low- and middle-income countries, to be more sustainable and that often requires more vigorous family-planning programmes.

The comfortably habitable zone is shrinking. It can be maintained with adaptation and mitigation, but these are often expensive and slow moving. In the shorter term, people are sometimes forced to move from places of greater to lesser vulnerability. Climate refugees are becoming more apparent although the bulk of them are internally displaced. Displacement because of climate change may be a significant driver of population movement in the years to come. We may be witnessing a demographic reordering owing to the redistribution of the global population brought about by climate change.

DEMOGRAPHY OF A GLOBAL POLITICAL ECONOMY

There is a distinct geography to demographic profiles. Three regions can be identified with different demographic issues and opportunities and different policy options. The first is what can be called the *youthful countries* that are still at the earlier stages of the DT, with high birth rates and rapid population growth. Previously, much of the global South was in this category, but today it is limited to a relatively small number of countries, especially in central Africa and the Middle East. They include Egypt, Ethiopia, Nigeria and Pakistan. Their demography is linked to limited economic development, since rapid population growth tends to dampen the growth of per capita GDP. Very youthful populations have high health and education costs that reduce household savings while increasing government expenditure. Rapid population growth is also associated with slow wage growth, especially for the unskilled. With more children in each family, many parents have less money to invest in each child. There is also a circular causation of low economic growth leading to lack of investment in education and infrastructure that can in turn reduce economic growth. We should note that it is not the demography that creates poverty or lack of economic growth. There is a long history of global economic and political exploitation that has reinforced inequalities in economic growth. It is not the demography that creates the poverty but more often it is the poverty that creates this demography.

For the young people in these societies there are limited economic opportunities. There are many reasons behind the new immigration flows, formal and informal, from Africa and the Middle East into Europe. Political instability and social conflict all play a role. But an underlying force behind waves of immigrants looking for a better life in Europe or North America is the lack of economic opportunity at home and the promise of better opportunities abroad.

In decades to come these young countries will experience a youth bulge and then a demographic dividend. Figure 9.1 shows the rapid population growth of Africa from 2020, compared to the continuing decline of Europe's population and the inflection point of Asia's population by 2050. By 2100, Africa's population is expected to be similar in size to Asia's population. The youth bulge may pose some issues of political stability, especially if a large mass of unemployed and underemployed young people is unable to find employment. And in a classic case of "exit/voice", this can lead to large-scale emigration abroad and/or protest and contestation at home. The coming demographic dividend of many people in the more economically productive age categories holds out the promise of rapid economic growth. Over the longer term, these more youthful countries could reap the benefit of a more favourable demography. But, as we have stressed repeatedly, the dividend is a possibility not a guarantee. It requires a range of policies that maximize and mobilize the growing working-age population in productive and sustainable ways.

The second group consists of *maturing countries* that are in the middle stages of the transition and that have a combination of youth bulges turning into demographic dividends. They include Brazil, India, Indonesia, Mexico

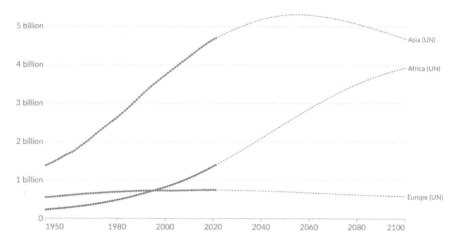

Figure 9.1 Population projections for Africa, Asia and Europe

Source: United Nations, World Population Prospects (2022), https://ourworldindata.org/grapher/population-with-un-projections?country= Africa+%28UN%29~Asia+%28UN%29~Europe+%28UN%29. Licensed under CC BY; Fig 9.2 Licensed under CC BY.

and Vietnam. These countries have had impressive growth rates with the possibility of more to come because of the large working-age population and the relatively smaller number of those aged under 15 and over 64. Theoretically, the demographic dividend works in several ways: an increase in the labour supply and the possibility of increasing productivity can absorb more workers; a decline in the number of dependents may increase the availability of capital to be invested in education and infrastructure that in turn can generate extra economic growth. Lower fertility rates allow women to devote more time to activities other than just having and rearing children and families can devote more resources to the education and training of individual children. This demographic context can result in the virtuous cycle of higher incomes leading to greater demand for goods and services that in turn generates more income. Policies that encourage education training and full labour force participation turn the possibility of a dividend into a reality. The demographic dividend has given these countries the basis for rapid economic growth. However, the demographic sweet spot does not last forever. The population ages. The task for these countries is to maximize the potential of the dividend as much as possible before, like contemporary China, they transition out into an ageing population and slowing growth.

Then there are the *ageing countries*. They include Finland, Greece, Italy, Japan, Russia and the UK, with China soon to join this category. These countries have ageing populations and an associated slowing of economic growth. Many of them are also starting, or will soon start, to lose population. A declining population has significant impacts on economic growth, with the possibility of decreased income per capita and implications for the solvency of social welfare funding. Economic decline is not inevitable. Policies that encourage full labour participation for as long as people want to work, greater utilization of the shrinking labour force and the immigration of skilled workers can all play a role in creating a silver economy. There is also the possibility of a second demographic dividend and even a depopulation dividend, which could include reductions in resource consumption, less pollution, greater biodiversity and improved work conditions.

There is also a political character to ageing societies. It is not a coincidence that many of these countries share similar political manifestations of populist nostalgia. A combustible combination of declining economies, greying populations and new streams of immigrants is creating a volatile politics conducive to the rise of authoritarian populism and nationalist xenophobia.

DEMOGRAPHY AND GEOPOLITICS

Nation states vary in power projection, from minor through major states to great powers. Demography plays a role in this hierarchy. A large population forms the basis of power projection, although having a large population does not guarantee great power status. Economic strength and military prowess also play a part in the power projection of states. The population base can also be spread widely for imperial powers. The UK, for example, was never the largest country in the world, either by territorial extent or by population size, but it was able to mobilize a much larger population and resource bases from its far-flung protectorates and colonies to become the superpower of the nineteenth century. British military power could draw upon the manpower of India, Canada, Australia and New Zealand among others to make it a global military force.

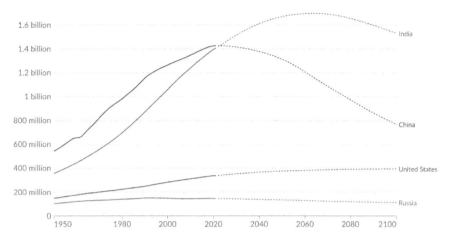

Figure 9.2 Population projections for China, India, Russia and the USA
Source: United Nations, World population Prospects (2022),
https://ourworldindata.org/grapher/population-with-un-projections?country =
CHN ~ IND ~ USA ~ RUS.

We can look at the demographic issues that underlie geopolitics in the contemporary world by considering China, India, Russia and the USA (see Figure 9.2).

China

China has always had a relatively large population compared to other countries in the world. However, its recent emergence as a global economic superpower emerged after 1979 with a combination of two factors. The first was a shift towards a more market-driven society that loosened the shackles of central planning and allowed market forces to flourish. There was also the demographic dividend of an increasing number of working-age adults. Between 1982 and 2002 the demographic dividend alone accounted for approximately 15 per cent of China's spectacular economic growth. The dividend was still in operation from 2002 to 2011 but at a reduced rate as the population began to age. China's working-age population peaked in 2011 at 900 million and will decline to 700 million by 2050. At the same time the number of Chinese aged

60 and over will increase from 200 million in 2022 to 500 million by 2050. China's window of demographic dividend is now closed.

Demographic trends can limit the power of states and hence their ability to project power on the regional and global stage. China is faced with demographic headwinds caused by a low birth rate, rapidly ageing population and declining working-age population. At present each retiree is supported by five workers but by 2050 it will be by two workers only.

After a population peak of 1.42 billion in 2021, China's population may dwindle to fewer than 800 million by the end of the century with more alarming scenarios putting the figure at fewer than 500 million. China's population will decline dramatically because of the unfolding effects of the one-child policy as well as historically low birth rates. Chinese women and especially educated women in cities seem reluctant to have more children.

By the end of this century China will have a higher old-age dependency ratio – the proportion of the population aged 65+ as a percentage of the working population aged 15–64 – than Japan, Germany, the UK, the USA and India. With a smaller working-age population, wages will tend to rise and China may lose its comparative advantage in the global economy. China also has to deal with the problem of millions more men than women, many of them from disadvantaged rural backgrounds.

In the coming decades China will face raising healthcare costs and tougher conditions for the elderly, especially in rural areas. Residents in the countryside receive a monthly pension of only $26 compared to over $500 for those living in the cities. There is also a two-tier healthcare system, with citizens in rural areas receiving very little state help while the main urban pension fund that covers 450 million urban workers residents will run dry by 2035. The transient underclass of 500 million migrant workers receives very little care. Policy attempts to raise the retirement age come up against the interests of urban middle class who represent a crucial base of support for the CCP. While the CCP has successfully managed rapid economic growth and created a huge new middle class, they have botched family planning. After the coercive one-child policy, China responded very slowly to new conditions. Authorities have known since the 1990s that the fertility rate was below replacement level yet only in 2016 did Beijing relax its one-child policy. China's TFR is now estimated to be 1.18 children per woman and official encouragement to increase birth rates is ineffectual as more Chinese women decide to have fewer children. In the decades to come China will face a demographic crisis with fewer workers, a burgeoning retirement population needing costly support and tremendous burdens on the one-child generation supporting four grandparents.

The demographic crisis along with the economic slowdown may be a cause for geopolitical concern as China, especially under President Xi, may perceive its window of opportunity for more aggressive behaviour towards the USA as coming to an end. Great powers are often more assertive, and more disruptive of the global order, when they perceive their own weakness compared to when they imagine their growing strength. By 2050 China may have 200 million fewer people than it does today, and the median age will climb from 38 years to 50. A shrinking and greying population presents political challenges for the increasingly autocratic regime of Xi. The legitimacy of CCP rule is in large measure based on economic performance and China's standing in the world. As growth slows, emphasis may be placed on a more aggressive nationalism. A mixture of an ageing population and the rigid political system does not bode well for China's global ambitions. This is not to say that demography will doom China or automatically undercut its current great power status. But the main rival to the USA will face strong demographic headwinds.

India

India's entrance to the global stage as an economic and military power is part because of the huge population and the benefits of a large demographic dividend. India has a working-age population that by 2040 may exceed 200 million. Since 2020 India's population has surpassed that of China. For the next 50 years India's population will continue to increase, and by 2100 India's population is estimated to be roughly 1.5 billion compared to China's 800 million. It is not just the size of the population but the nature of the population that is important in determining economic strength. India is much better placed in this regard compared to say China and Russia, not only because it has a large and growing population but also because it stands to benefit from a massive demographic dividend, with a population much younger than either Russia or China. India can look forward to a productive demographic future with a long-lasting demographic dividend while that of China and Russia is bleaker. India will be the world's third largest economy by 2030.

We should be careful, however, in using the term India or indeed any other in individual country as a single, coherent demographic unit. There are different trajectories inside India. In the southern state of Tamil Nadu, for example, average women will have 1.8 children but in Bihar and the north the average is three children per woman. There are in fact two Indias: one in the south that resembles East Asia and one in the north that looks more like central Africa. The north is the heartland of support for the Hindu nationalist Bharatiya Janata Party party.

We should be wary of using different demographic profiles to draw too straight a line between the decline of China and the rise of India. India does have certain advantages, with a massive demographic dividend and a largely rules-based constitutional order. However, India is a fractious, rambunctious democracy that finds it difficult at times to develop the infrastructure, reform the regulations and improve the basic welfare services that would allow the full flowering of the demographic dividend. Its more contentious politics often makes it more difficult to undergo the rapid modernization of its more autocratic East Asian neighbours.

India's growth potential is weakened by a growing religious divide and a vast informal sector. India has consistently failed to provide enough jobs to keep up with its growing population and the result is a vast informal sector that underutilizes the country's economic potential. There is also still some uncertainty for foreign direct investors due a long tradition of protectionist policies. Entry into the Indian market is made difficult by tariffs on foreign-made components. There is also the fact that despite the large population, the market of middle-class consumers remains only around 15 per cent of the population. There is a bachelor bomb of 37 million surplus men for whom the lack of female partners and the lessening possibilities of marriage, combined with unemployment and economic marginalization, has created a toxic stew of frustrated masculinity that is a powerful force behind the right-wing nationalist sense of victimhood that often targets Muslims, women and the lower classes.

While India has now the world's largest population, and its huge demographic dividend will allow it to become a major economic and military force with a growing role in global geopolitics, it still has major issues because of a lack of jobs and limited human development for much of its population. Despite the problems, India is setting itself up to become the effective leader of the global South.

Russia

In 1989 the USSR was the third most populous country in the world, with its almost 250 million inhabitants constituting over 5.5 per cent of the world's population. Russia emerged from the dismemberment of the Soviet Union after losing the territory of the former Soviet Republics. Its population shrunk to 148 million with millions of Russian speakers left in newly independent countries such as Ukraine and the new Baltic states. By 2023 the population of Russia had fallen to 144 million (142 million excluding Crimea) and slipped to the ninth most populous. The sense of population loss on top of the troubling demographic issues of an ageing population feed into what some commentators refer to as a post-imperial syndrome. The decline of empire involves a sense of loss of self-importance that gives rise to resentment followed by a thirst for revenge and the commitment to restore the status quo of great power status. This is now manifest in Russia where the sense of loss of great power status is heightened by a shrunken and declining population, territorial diminution and the stranding of Russian speakers in now foreign lands. The syndrome is expressed in a sense of a Russia under threat from the West. Under Putin, Russia has embarked on reclaiming its historical position through the illegal acquisition of territory. The annexation of Crimea in 2014 and the war on Ukraine, which began in 2022, were part of Putin's mission to return Russia to the great power status it lost after the fall of the USSR. There are many reasons behind Putin's expansionist and dangerous geopolitics but the sense of loss of imperial greatness is paramount.

The syndrome is exacerbated by Russia's demographic woes. Russia's population peaked in 1993 at 148.6 million. Since then, it has experienced a 2 per cent decline compared to a 28 per cent increase for the USA for roughly the same period. Life expectancy for men in Russia is only 66 compared to almost 75 in the USA. And with a birth rate of 1.5 children per woman the population decline will continue. Its population is characterized by very low birth rates and a declining and ageing population. The death rate has exceeded the birth rate every year from 1992 to 2023 with only a brief respite from 2012 to 2016. Russia's economic strength is almost entirely based on its exports of minerals and fossil fuels, especially oil and gas, to China and Europe. This is too narrow a base to build a sustainable economy and makes the country's finances dependent on volatile markets. Russia's problems include limited human capital investment. Although it has high levels of schooling it has low levels of human capital, defined as the skills and expertise possessed by individuals, something referred to as the Russian paradox. Russia's working-age population will diminish from now until 2040. The country's human capital has diminished even more since the invasion of Ukraine started, when between half a million and a million young, educated Russians left the country to avoid compulsory military conscription.

The invasion of Ukraine can be seen as an attempt to recreate both imperial grandeur and demographic heft. It is the Russian version of post-imperial syndrome The combination of perceived geopolitical decline and actual demographic shrinkage is a crucial part of the background to Putin's ill-fated decision to invade Ukraine.

United States

Part of the rise of the USA to superpower status was its surging population. In 1850, the United States was home to only 23 million people, 13 million fewer than France. Today, the US population is close to 330 million while that of France is close to 65 million. There are many reasons behind America's rise to global dominance, but its hefty demographic base is one of them. A large population base is often a requirement of great power status. Raw population numbers are important but so is the quality of human capital. Compared to China, India and Russia, the US has a well-educated population. For each additional year of schooling a country sees on average a 10 per cent increase in per capita GDP.

The US has certain demographic advantages. First, there is the size of its population and the amount of investment in human capital, especially compared to its rivals. There is an American demographic exceptionalism which is the fact that the USA, compared to other rich countries, has a younger population because of higher birth rates and immigration levels. The USA will have more births than deaths until 2040.

In the arena of geopolitical competition many of the allies of the USA, especially in Europe, face the demographic challenges of low birth rates and ageing populations that act as a drag on military power. In the longer term, the USA may have to rely more on alliances and partnerships with the new demographic powerhouses such India, Indonesia and the Philippines, which have respective populations of 1.42 billion, 300 million and 118 million, to maintain its global supremacy. A pivot to Asia is a demographic necessity for US designs in the Pacific. It will also need to devote more attention to a demographically surging Africa.

As the USA faces off against China and addresses the possible superpower rivalry, both countries need big populations and economic growth to sustain their competitive advantage. The USA has the advantages of a relatively large population with a much higher per capita GDP than its geopolitical rivals, China and Russia. It faces no immediate demographic crisis, although the ageing of the population will accelerate as births decline. However, it faces more pressing and immediate problems of internal cohesion, unfunded government spending and increasing inequality that slows down economic growth and exacerbates social tensions. At home, the country needs to improve its human capital base, and overseas it must forge economic ties and military alliance with the new demographic powerhouses such as India, Philippines and Indonesia and a population surging Africa.

SUMMARY

Demographic changes are tightly bound with some of the major global challenges. Climate change is impacted by population in two ways. First, the steady increase in the world population generates a greater carbon footprint and puts extra pressure on the world's resources. And in association with increasing affluence and greater technological impact, the effect is an increase in greenhouse gases, which in turn has led to a significant enough warming of the planet to influence future population distribution. Today's climate refugees may be the initial stage in significant population redistributions. More people, including those in large cities of the global South, island populations and coastal populations are now more at risk from the extreme events associated with climate change. Global warming also involves the shrinking of the biosphere and its greater vulnerability to extreme climate events.

There is a global population shift in process. By 2050 one in every four people in the world will live in Africa. Africa has the greatest potential for future demographic dividends. Almost 60 per cent of Africa's population is aged under 25 and the median age is only 20. In Europe and North America, the median age is closer to 40. In many African countries there is a growing age gap between ageing political elites and a very youthful citizenry. While some fear that this youth bulge may destabilize these low-income countries, it has also brought waves of protest that have resisted authoritarian and undemocratic regimes. While not all have achieved functioning democracies, democratization is often the result of years of unarmed, democratic mobilization.

Assuming a medium fertility scenario the world's population will continue to rise from its current eight billion and level off at just over ten billion in 2080. Behind this global figure lies substantial differences. By 2100, eight out of ten people will live in Asia or Africa. The population of low-income countries will continue to rise from around one billion today to over two billion at the end of the century. The population of Africa will increase from roughly 1.5 billion to 4 billion. The population of higher-income countries will remain static or decline. The population of countries such as Albania, Bulgaria, Croatia, Finland, Greece and Serbia have already started to decline. The population of Croatia is currently around four million and is likely to decrease to only two million by the end of the century. Serbia's population decline is from roughly eight million today to just over three million by the end of the century. China's population is likely to fall from over 1.4 billion to just under 800 million. Brazil's population will level off around 2040 from almost 250 million to under 200 million. In other words, there will be a substantial redistribution of population, with the demographic centre of gravity shifting towards Africa and away from Europe and East Asia. Population shifts on their own do not automatically herald global reshufflings. But as the population centre of gravity shifts to South and Southeast Asia and Africa the continuing economic dominance of Europe and the USA may not be assured.

There is a demographic basis to contemporary geopolitics. India's economic and military rise is in part because of its burgeoning population and huge demographic dividend. Demography can also eat away at great power status. The ageing populations of Russia and China constrain their economies and hence their great power projection. The perceived threat of a demographic crisis, such as in China and Russia, may also prompt authoritarian leaders to look for ways to project power through more muscular foreign policies and more threatening military postures. A sense of population decline may be one reason behind Putin's strategy of invading Ukraine and China's aggressive policies towards its neighbours. Authoritarian and even democratically elected leaders often look to foreign venture to buttress domestic support and stifle internal criticisms. Demography is not the only reason for great power status and demographic decline is not the only reason behind more aggressive foreign policy posture, but they can play a significant role as demographic decline can be read by great power leaders as a symbol of national decline. It is a reminder of the major theme that runs through all the discussions in this book. Demography is a vital force in contemporary events but is not a predetermined destiny. It is not a given but both an opportunity and a challenge.

FURTHER READING

Eberstadt, N. 2023. "With great demographics comes great power". *Foreign Affairs*. https://www.foreignaffairs.com/articles/africa/2021-07-07/promise-africas-youth-bulge.

Garbuzov, V. 2022. "Zigzags of the post-imperial syndrome". *European Studies* 92: S492–503.

Leatherby, L. 2023. "How a vast demographic shift will reshape the globe". *New York Times*. https://www.nytimes.com/interactive/2023/07/16/world/world-demographics.html.

Mampilly, M. 2021. "The promise of Africa's youth bulge". *Foreign Affairs*. https://www.foreignaffairs.com/articles/africa/2021-07-07/promise-africas-youth-bulge.

Turner II, B. 2023. *The Anthropocene: 101 Questions and Answers for Understanding the Human Impact on the Global Environment*. Newcastle upon Tyne: Agenda Publishing.

References

Abot, E. 2014. *Istorija braka* [History of Marriage]. Beograd, Serbia: Geopoetika.

Abramitzky, R., A. Delavande & L. Vasconcelos 2011. "Marrying up: the role of sex ratio in assertive matching". *American Economic Journal: Applied Economics* 3(3): 124–57.

Adebowale, A. 2019. "Ethnic disparities in fertility and its determinants in Nigeria". *Fertility Research and Practice* 5: 3.

Ahmed, S. *et al.* 2016. "How significant is sub-Saharan Africa's demographic dividend for its future growth and poverty reduction?". *Review of Development Economics* 20(4): 762–93.

Ashraf, Q. & O. Galor 2013. "The 'Out of Africa' hypothesis, human genetic diversity, and comparative economic development". *American Economic Review* 103: 1–46.

Benton, M. *et al.* 2021. "The influence of evolutionary history on human health and disease". *Nature Reviews Genetics* 22: 269–83.

Blom, P. 2019. *Nature's Mutiny: How the Little Ice Age of the Long Seventeenth Century Transformed the West and Shaped the Present*. New York: Liveright Publishing.

Buck v. Bell 1927. Oyez 274 US 200. www.oyez.org/cases/1900-1940/274us200.

Büntgen, U. *et al.* 2016. "Cooling and societal change during the Late Antique Little Ice Age from 536 to around 660 AD". *Nature Geosciences* 9: 231–6.

Dang, H. & F. Rogers 2016. "The decision to invest in child quality over quantity: household size and household investment in education in Vietnam". *World Bank Economic Review* 30(1): 104–42.

Diamond-Smith, N. & K. Rudolph 2018. "The association between uneven sex ratios and violence: evidence from 6 Asian countries". *PLoS ONE* 13(6): e0197516.

Dotti, V. 2020. "No country for young people? The rise of anti-immigration populism in aging societies". https://mpra.ub.uni-muenchen.de/100226/1/MPRA_paper_100226.pdf.

Edlund, L. *et al.* 2013. "Sex ratios and crime: evidence from China". *Review of Economics and Statistics* 95(5): 1520–34.

Farfaras, A. *et al.* 2016. "The Greek economic crisis leads to declining birth rates". *International Journal of Child Health and Human Development* 9(2): 157–62.

Fernández-López de Pablo, J. *et al.* 2019. "Palaeodemographic modelling supports a population bottleneck during the Pleistocene–Holocene transition in Iberia". *Nature Communications* 10: 1872.

Flueckiger, M. & M. Ludwig 2018. "Youth bulges and civil conflict: causal evidence from sub-Saharan Africa". *Journal of Conflict Resolution* 69(9): 1932–62.

Fuller, G. & F. Pitts 1990. "Youth cohorts and political unrest in South Korea". *Political Geography Quarterly* 9(1): 9–22.

Golestaneh, L. *et al.* 2020. "The association of race and COVID-19 mortality". *EClinicalMedicine* 25: 100455.

Greenhalgh, S. 2009. "The Chinese biopolitical: facing the twenty-first century". *New Genetics and Society* 28: 205–22.

Grier, K., D. Hicks & W. Yuan 2016. "Marriage matching and conspicuous consumption in China". *Economic Inquiry* 54(2): 1251–62.

Heinsohn, G. 2021. "Youth bulge und das gewaltpotential junger männer". In *Jahrbuch des Instituts für Angewandte Forschung 2020*. https://www.nomos-elibrary.de/10.5771/9783415069473/jahrbuch-des-instituts-fuer-angewandte-forschung-2020#page=234.

Hernandez, A. 2023. "In graying Puerto Rico, the elderly faced climate disasters alone". *Washington Post*, 13 January. https://www.washingtonpost.com/nation/2023/01/13/puerto-rico-hurricanes-climate-elderly/.

Huntington, S. 2011. *The Clash of Civilizations and the Remaking of World Order*. New York: Simon & Schuster.

Jett, J. 2023. "China's population falls for first time in decades hampering its economic rise". NBC News, 17 January. https://www.nbcnews.com/news/world/chinas-population-declines-first-time-decades-rcna65928.

Kearney, M. & P. Levine 2022. "The causes and consequences of declining US fertility". Aspen Institute. https://www.economicstrategygroup.org/publication/kearney_levine/.

Keys, D. 2000. *Catastrophe: An Investigation into the Origins of the Modern World*. New York: Ballantine.

Klunk, J. *et al.* 2022. "Evolution of immune genes is associated with the Black Death". *Nature* 611: 312–19.

La Ferrara, E., A. Chong & S. Duryea 2012. "Soap operas and fertility: evidence from Brazil". *American Economic Journal: Applied Economics* 4: 1–31.

Lesthaeghe, R. 1977. *The Decline of Belgian Fertility 1800–1970*. Princeton, NJ: Princeton University Press.

Lesthaeghe, R. 2010. "The unfolding story of the second demographic transition". *Population and Development Review* 36(2): 211–51.

Lesthaeghe, R. & A. Lopez-Gay 2013. "Spatial continuities and discontinuities in two successive demographic transitions: Spain and Belgium, 1880–2010". *Demographic Research* 28: 77–136.

Lu, S. 2019. *The Making of Settler Colonialism*. Cambridge: Cambridge University Press.

Lynch, K. 2003. *Individuals, Families, and Communities in Europe, 1200–1800: The Urban Foundations of Western Society*. Cambridge: Cambridge University Press.

Marcus, A., M. Islam & J. Moloney 2008. "Youth bulges, busts, and doing business in violence-prone nations". *Business and Politics* 10(3): 1–40.

REFERENCES

Matloubkari, E. & B. Shaikh Baikloo Islam 2022. "Climate change and challenges of the last ancient dynasty of Iran: the decline and fall of the Sassanid empire". *Persica Antiqua* 2: 61–76.

McCurry, J. 2022. "Record number of young people in Japan rejecting marriage, says report". *The Guardian*, 14 September. https://www.theguardian.com/world/2022/sep/14/record-number-of-young-people-in-japan-rejecting-marriage-survey-shows.

Newman, S. 2017. "Infanticide". *Aeon*. https://aeon.co/essays/the-roots-of-infanticide-run-deep-and-begin-with-poverty.

Office of National Statistics 2022. "Health state life expectancies by national deprivation deciles, England: 2018 to 2020". https://www.ons.gov.uk/peoplepopulationandcommunity/healthandsocialcare/healthinequalities/bulletins/healthstatelifeexpectanciesbyindexofmultipledeprivationimd/2018to2020.

Olivetti, C. & B. Petrongolo 2017. "The economic consequences of family policies: lessons from a century of legislation in high-income countries". *Journal of Economic Perspectives* 31(1): 205–30.

Parker, G. 2013. *Global Crisis: War, Climate Change and Catastrophe in the Seventeenth Century*. New Haven, CT: Yale University Press.

Roser, M. 2014. "Fertility Rate". https://ourworldindata.org/fertility-rate.

Schacht, R. & K. Kramer 2016. "Patterns of family formation in response to sex ratio variation". *PLoS ONE* 11(8): 1–14.

Schwandt, H. & T. von Wachter 2019. "Unlucky cohorts: estimating the long-term effects of entering the labor market in a recession in large cross-sectional data sets". *Journal of Labor Economics* 37(S1): S161–98.

Seligson, K. 2023. *The Maya and Climate Change*. New York: Oxford University Press.

Shu, X. & Y. Ye 2022. "Misfortune of children of the Cultural Revolution: cohort size, historical times, and life chances in China". In Y. Li & Y. Bian (eds), *Social Inequality in China*, 131–55. Singapore: World Scientific.

Smith, T. 2023. "The greatest wealth transfer in history is here with familiar (rich) winners". *New York Times*, 23 May. https://www.nytimes.com/2023/05/14/business/economy/wealth-generations.html.

Szreter, S. 1993. "The idea of demographic transition and the study of fertility change: a critical intellectual history". *Population and Development Review* 19: 659–701.

Tallavaara, M. *et al.* 2015. "Population dynamics in Europe over the last glacial maximum". *Proceedings of the National Academy of Sciences USA* 112: 8232–7.

Thornton, R. 1987. *American Indian Holocaust and Survival: A Population History since 1492*. Norman: University of Oklahoma Press.

Trost, S. *et al.* 2022. "Pregnancy-related deaths: data from Maternal Mortality Review Committees in 36 US states, 2017–2019". Centers for Disease Control and Prevention. https://www.cdc.gov/reproductivehealth/maternal-mortality/erase-mm/data-mmrc.html.

Turner II, B. 2020. "The ancient Maya response to climate change: a cautionary tale". *Harvard Gazette*. https://news.harvard.edu/gazette/story/2020/02/new-clues-about-how-and-why-the-maya-culture-collapsed/.

UK Government 2017. "Health profile for England". https://www.gov.uk/government/publications/health-profile-for-england/chapter-5-inequality-in-health.

Urdal, H. 2006. "A clash of generations? Youth bulges and political violence". *International Studies Quarterly* 50(3): 607–29.

Urdal, H. & K. Hoelscher 2009. "Urban youth bulges and social disorder: an empirical study of Asian and sub-Saharan African cities". World Bank Policy Research Working Paper 5110.

US Census 2022. "Historical World Population". https://www.census.gov/data/tables/time-series/demo/international-programs/historical-est-worldpop.html.

Wrigley, E. & R. Schofield 1989. *The Population History of England 1541–1871*. Cambridge: Cambridge University Press.

Wrigley, E., R. Davies, J. Oeppen & R. Schofield 1997. *English Population History from Family Reconstitution 1580–1837*. Cambridge: Cambridge University Press.

Yair, O. & D. Miodownik 2016. "Youth bulge and civil war: why a country's share of young adults explains only non-ethnic wars". *Conflict Management & Peace Science* 33(1): 25–44.

Zhang, J. 2017. "The evolution of China's one-child policy and its effects on family outcomes". *Journal of Economic Perspectives* 31(1): 141–60.

Index

abortion   52, 57, 90, 97, 99, 100, 102, 105
Achilles   28
Afghanistan   52–4, 68
Africa
   demographic dividend   82, 150
   population   2, 14, 38, 47, 54, 149–50, 159–60
   youth bulge   54, 69–70, 82, 150
   urbanization   38
age cohorts   7, 52, 76, 82
ageing
   China   60, 77, 93–5, 123, 152, 155, 160
   countries   152
   compression   114–16
   economic effects   116–20
   Japan   77, 115–16
   population   1, 67, 83, 92, 107–109, 116, 119, 120, 124–9 154, 157–60
   societies   3, 123, 137–9, 152,
agricultural revolution   33–4, 39
Anthropocene   147–8
Arab Spring   2, 70–72, 138
Arabian Peninsula   18
Asia   22, 69, 101, 128, 159, 160
   East Asia   73, 77, 82, 108, 156
   Northeast Asia   48
   South Asia   38, 73, 75, 77, 82

Athens   16–17
Australia   14, 47–8, 94, 118, 152

bachelor bomb   75–6, 84, 156
Bangladesh   80, 81, 88, 114, 148
   demographic dividend   80
   fertility rate   80
Belgium   6
Bering Strait   15
biopolitics   31, 33, 38–40, 49
birth rates   7–9, 39, 43, 47, 51–7, 65, 77, 83–4, 87, 92, 96, 102–105, 107, 117, 120, 128, 132, 136, 140, 145, 149
Black Death   19–24, 27
Boserup, Esther   133
Brazil   2, 48, 56, 69, 77, 83, 88, 148, 150
   birth rate   88
   demographic dividend   77, 83
   telenovelas   56
Britain   31, 48, 123, 126, 138
Brooklyn   38, 50
Burkina Faso   44

Camus, Renaud   135
Central African Republic   45
child labour   37
child mortality   36, 44, 45, 46, 52, 65

Afghanistan 52
Burkina Faso 44
Central African Republic 45
Iceland 45
USA 45
China 23, 29, 56–60, 65, 74–5, 77, 93, 94–6, 100, 123–4, 132, 140, 141, 152–60
   abortion 100
   age cohorts 76
   ageing 59, 77, 94, 123–4, 152
   birth rate 93, 100, 124, 140, 154
   demographic crisis 155, 159
   demographic dividend 77
   family planning 56–60
   gender disparity 59, 74–5
   one child policy 29, 57, 60, 65, 132,
   second demographic dividend 153–4
Christianity 28
climate change 3, 24, 134, 147–9, 159
Coale, Anlsey 10
Cohen, Stanley 138
cohorts 7–8, 52, 73–8, 80, 82, 84, 90, 104, 131, 138–9
Cold War 10
Comte, Auguste 2
contraception 50–52, 55–8, 60–65, 89, 90–91, 98–9, 105, 132
Covid-19 15, 112–13
Crohn's disease 22

death rates 7–8, 15, 17, 39, 43, 77, 112–13
demographic bulge 9
demographic crisis 139, 155, 160
demographic dividend 3, 67, 72, 77–84, 87, 93, 95, 150, 151, 155–6,160
   second demographic dividend 120, 128, 152
   silver demographic dividend 120
Demographic Holocaust 15, 22
demographic narratives 131
demographic transition 2, 5
   second demographic transition 102
demography 1–3, 6, 13, 24, 28, 31, 36, 38–9, 62, 82, 84, 103–104, 119, 131, 134, 140, 144, 147, 149–50, 152, 155 160–61

as destiny 2, 82, 140
ageing population 119
climate change 147
geopolitics 152, 160–61
global political economy 149–50
dependency ratio 54, 64–5, 67, 77, 80–81, 109, 118, 121, 154
   Bangladesh 80
   China 154
   Japan 118
   Nigeria 64–5
   USA 121

Easterlin, Richard 76
Egypt 68, 70–71, 149
   family planning 149
   youth bulge 68, 70–71
Ehrlich, Paul 131–3
Ehrlich, Anne 131, 133
El Salvador 88
England 5, 6, 19, 23, 27, 30, 36, 47, 96,
   birth rates 96
   life expectancy 27
   and Wales 33, 44
eugenics 49–51, 65
Europe 2, 6, 7, 16, 19–20, 22, 30, 32, 35, 48, 65, 77, 93, 101, 108, 109, 113, 115, 118, 126, 135, 136, 137, 141, 148, 150, 157, 158, 160

family planning 10, 49–52, 55, 56, 57, 60–65, 149
   China 57
   Egypt 149
   India 56, 62–3
   Nigeria 63–5
   Philippines 61–2, 65
   Sanger, Margaret 50–52
   Thailand 60–61
family values 131, 140, 142, 145
famine 5, 13, 18, 23, 30, 32, 57, 132–3
female labour participation rates 40, 101, 116
fertility rate 5–7, 10, 47, 56, 57–9, 61, 63, 80, 89–90, 97, 98, 100, 103, 121, 149, 154

INDEX

Bangladesh   80
China   57–9, 61, 100, 154
Egypt   149
global   5
India   56
Nigeria   63
Norway   6
Russia   97
Scotland   47
USA   89–90, 103, 121
USSR   98
food supply   15, 16, 30–32, 34, 39–40, 132–4
Ford Foundation   55
Foucault, Michel   38
France   19, 78, 96, 115, 123, 136, 14, 142, 158,
  life expectancy   78
  retirement policy   123

Galton, Francis   49
gender bulge   67, 84
gender imbalance   73, 76
genetic diversity   14–15
genetic legacy   13, 21
Germany   32, 50, 107–108, 114, 115, 118, 123, 154
  ageing   107–108, 114
Global North   9, 36–8, 43–4, 46–7, 52, 54–5, 65
global political economy   149
Global South   10, 36, 38, 43–6, 48, 52, 54–5, 63, 65, 77, 132, 135, 144, 149, 156, 159
Godwin, William   32
Grant, Michael   36
Greece   18, 91, 107, 112, 115, 123, 128, 152, 160
green revolution   40
Guillard, Achille   1

Heinsohn, Gunnar   68
Himmler, Herbert   50
Hitler, Adolf   32
Hobbes, Thomas   27
Holmes, Oliver Wendell   50

Hoover, Edgar M.   10
Huntington, Samuel   72

Ice Age   16, 18, 23–4, 27, 33
  late antiquity   18
  Little Ice Age   23–4, 27, 33
Iceland   45, 141
illegitimacy   141–2, 144–5
immigration   2, 48, 52, 78, 92–4, 107, 109, 116–28, 136–8, 145, 150–52, 158
India   2, 10, 55–7, 62, 63, 74, 75, 77, 80–81, 83, 132, 150, 152–6, 158, 159
  bachelor bomb   156
  demographic dividend   77, 81, 83, 150, 155
  family planning   55, 56, 62–3
  fertility rates   56–7, 63, 74, 156
  sterilization program   55, 132
Industrial Revolution   23–4, 33–4
infant mortality   7–9, 16, 27–8, 43–6, 63–4, 67, 88, 99, 132
Iran   99
Iraq   70
Irish Famine   47
Islam   18, 28, 64
Italy   52, 88, 107–108, 109, 114–15, 122–3, 128, 152
  ageing   107, 109, 114, 122–3

Jamaica   67
Japan   2, 46, 48, 52, 54, 65, 68, 77, 78, 81, 88, 92, 101, 102, 107, 108, 109, 112, 114–16, 118, 120, 125, 128, 137, 141, 152, 154
  ageing   77, 115–16
  birth rate   101, 102, 120

Korea   28
Krakatoa   14

labour participation rates   40
life expectancy   1, 3, 5, 6, 8, 13, 27, 30, 39, 46, 64, 65, 73, 76–8, 87–8, 93, 109–14, 119–21, 123, 148, 157
Little Ice Age   23–5, 27, 33
longevity economy   119–22

169

Mali 6, 54
Malthus, Thomas 30–32, 39–40, 132, 134, 144
Malthusian 30, 33, 40, 47–8, 66, 133, 144
marriage 5, 7, 9, 59, 64, 73, 75, 79, 84, 91, 96, 118, 140–42, 145, 156
Maya 18–19
Mayan Collapse 18
Mexico 6, 18, 141, 150
Middle East 149, 150
Middle East and North Africa (MENA) 70
moral panics 3, 131, 144–5
mortality rate 43–5, 47, 73, 112
mortality rates 3, 5, 7, 13, 36, 39, 43, 45, 48, 52, 65, 73, 88

national identicide 137
national identity 118 145
national population 62, 83, 95, 105, 135–7
national populations 105, 131, 137, 144
New World 15, 22, 24, 33, 47
Niger 52–4, 88, 107
Nigeria 6, 52, 63–5, 88, 149
  family planning 63–5
North Macedonia 115
Norway 6, 120, 141

overpopulation 95, 131, 132–4, 138, 144

patriarchal 28, 39, 56, 97
patriarchy 28–9, 140
Philippines 29, 61–2, 65, 81, 159
  family planning 61–2, 65
Pleistocene 16
population bottlenecks 13, 23
population decline 23, 27, 57, 59, 87, 92–5, 97, 100, 124, 157, 160
  China 57, 59, 93–5, 100, 124
  Russia 97
  Serbia 160
  USSR 97
population growth 3, 5, 8–10, 17, 27, 30–31, 38–40, 43, 46–9, 52–5, 57–61, 63–5, 87, 88, 93, 97, 99, 104, 105, 126, 128, 132–4, 144, 149, 150

population loss 13, 18, 23–4, 92, 157
population policies 55, 64
population profile 9, 52
population projections 135, 151, 153
population pyramid 7, 8, 67, 71, 74, 81, 108–109, 126, 145
Portugal 107, 115, 128
pronatalist 96–8, 100–102, 105
Puerto Rico 107, 114–15
  ageing 115
Pyrocene 147

Quebec 101
Queen Elizabeth 6
Queen Victoria 6

recession 21, 89, 90
recession scarring 76
retirement 94, 119–24, 126, 154–5
Rockefeller Foundation 55
Romania 99
Rostow model 10
Rousseau, Jean-Jacques 27
Russia 73, 76, 97, 98, 110, 152–3, 155, 157–60
  abortion 98
  birth rate 157
  family planning 97
  fertility rate 97

Sanger, Margaret 50–52
Sassanid Empire 18
Scotland 47
second demographic transition 11, 102, 120, 128, 144, 152
Sen, Amartya 133
Senegal 29
seniors 115, 120–21, 127
senior shift 127
settler colonialism 47, 48, 65
Siberia 15, 22
silver demographic dividend 120
silver economy 119, 152
silver tsunami 138–9
social Darwinism 32

INDEX

South Asia   38, 75, 77, 82
South Korea   70, 74, 77, 81, 88, 101, 108, 117–18, 127–8, 140–42
  birth rate   101, 107
Soviet Union   76, 97, 110, 157
  Birth rate   97
Spain   6, 68 101, 128
Spencer, Herbert   32
Sri Lanka   88
sterilization   50, 55, 58, 132, 136
sub-Saharan Africa   69, 82, 38

Taiwan   128
Thailand   60–61, 65
  family planning   60–61
Toba   14, 18
total fertility rate (TFR)   58, 87

UK   6, 32, 43–7, 52, 54, 72, 73, 88, 96, 119, 142, 152, 154
urbanization   10, 33, 35, 38, 40, 41, 59
United Nations   3, 17, 55, 108, 135, 151, 153
USA   2, 10, 32, 37, 44–8, 50–52, 54, 59, 70, 72–3, 76, 78, 89, 90–91, 93, 102–103, 108, 110, 112–14, 117–19, 121–2, 124, 126, 136, 139, 141–3, 148, 153–4, 156–60
  abortion   102, 119, 121
  ageing   108, 114, 122, 126, 139

birth rates   78, 89–91, 103, 158
child mortality   44, 45
dependency ratio   54, 121, 154
eugenics   50–51
fertility rate   89–90, 103, 121
illegitimacy   142
life expectancy   46, 73, 110, 112–14, 148, 157
maternal deaths   45
recession scaring   76
working-age population   93
USSR   97–8, 157
  abortion   97

Vietnam   36, 74, 77–8, 88, 151
  demographic dividend   77–8
Viking sagas   28
vital statistics   1

Wilson, E. O.   132
working-age population   54, 71, 77–8, 80, 82, 92–4, 116, 117, 121, 150–51, 153–5, 158
world population   3, 9, 14–18, 23, 159
World Bank   55, 64, 122

youth bulge   3, 67, 68–72, 77, 83, 84, 138, 145–6, 159–60
youth mortality   43, 45